LOVED by GOD

100 Days with Women in the Word

ZONDERVAN

Loved By God: 100 Days with Women in the Word

Published in Grand Rapids, Michigan, by Zonderkidz. Zonderkidz is a registered trademark of The Zondervan Corporation, L.L.C., a wholly owned subsidiary of HarperCollins Christian Publishing, Inc.

Requests for information should be addressed to customercare@harpercollins.com.

ISBN 978-0-310176060 (print)
ISBN 978-0310176084 (audio)
ISBN 978-310176077 (ebook)

Cover Design: Jamie DeBryun
Interior Design: Emily Ghattas
Written by Lindsay A. Franklin

Library of Congress Control Number: 2025937145

Printed in the United States of America

25 26 27 28 29 LBC 5 4 3 2 1

Introduction

It's hard to be a young woman. We're bombarded by lots of different messages about who we're supposed to be—and often, those messages contradict each other. So, what's the right path? Who do we listen to? Which messages should be filtered out and which should be embraced?

If we're followers of Jesus, we look to God's Word for answers. What does God think about the issues we face? What does he say about who we're supposed to be and how we're supposed to act? What does it mean to be a godly woman, anyway? God's Word has answers to all these questions and a whole lot more.

In the coming weeks, we'll see through the pages of Scripture that there are numerous ways to honor God in our lives. While it's true we all have different paths, one thing we all have in common is that we are loved by God. That's important to understand because if we know we are loved and valued by God, we won't be compelled to look for validation in empty things that don't have the ability to fulfill us.

Thankfully, the Bible has so much to teach us about what it means to live as a young woman loved by God. Scripture speaks to the heartaches and the high points of being female. There are dozens of women in the Bible, some named but many unnamed. We're going to look at many of them. Through their stories, we'll discover role models and cautionary tales, tragedies and triumphs. And guess what? The stories of these ancient women are relevant to our lives today.

Make no mistake, you are loved by God and your identity as a woman matters to God! So, let's see what his Word has to say about it.

Day 1

See what great love the Father has lavished on us, that we should be called children of God! And that is what we are!

1 JOHN 3:1

Some people think that the Bible is a "guys' book." A book written by men, about men, for men. That girls and women have little or no role in God's interaction with humankind. That we're afterthoughts. The truth is, God's Word is for all of us.

The Bible teaches that God loves us—both males and females—so much that he calls us children of God (1 John 1:3). You might be wondering how that is possible. After all, you can probably think of a long list of your sins and flaws. Maybe you don't even believe you're worthy of God's love. The truth is, that those of us who follow Jesus as Lord have been reconciled to the Father through Christ's death on the cross (Rom. 5:8). Everyone who acknowledges Jesus as Savior is a beloved child of God.

Our female examples in the Bible rarely fall into the two stereotypes so often foisted upon women in our culture—either virtuous angels or wicked seductresses. No, most women of the Bible are drawn in real, human shades of gray—sometimes

displaying good qualities, sometimes negative qualities, filled with wisdom as well as bad choices, walking in faith and stumbling in darkness. Just like the men of the Bible. *Just like us.*

Girls and women are not God's afterthoughts. We're his daughters. Valued. Adored. Cherished. Loved by God.

How does knowing you are loved by God make a difference in your life?

The Bible teaches that God loves us—both males and females—so much that he calls us children of God (1 John 1:3).

Day 2

Adam named his wife Eve,
because she would become
the mother of all the living.
GENESIS 3:20

Over the next several weeks, we're going to spend time in both the Old and New Testament learning about women in the Bible. And what better place to begin our look at the triumphs and trials of biblical women than with Eve, the first woman? Eve's name is derived from the Hebrew word meaning "to breathe" or the related word "to live." How cool is that? Breath and life, two words that bring to mind "vitality," and that's what Eve was. With Adam, she began human life.

Eve's story, more than perhaps any other biblical woman, represents the highest of highs and the lowest of lows. She alone of all women lived without sin for a while. Eve experienced the fullness of God's favor and his blessing. She was female kind as we were created to be. And only in understanding that can we fully appreciate the great tragedy of Eve's mistake.

Eve was deceived into disobeying God's one command (Gen. 3:5–6). She broke a rule that probably felt so small at

the time—a mere tiptoe away from the Father and toward her own desires. Just one bite. But that tiptoe sparked catastrophic results. In Eve, we have both our first role model and our saddest cautionary tale. Eve's story points us toward our need for a Savior (John 14:6).

Just like Eve—and everyone who has ever lived—we have sinned against God (Rom. 3:23). But the good news is, God still loves us even when we've sinned (Rom. 5:8). And we can find forgiveness for our sins through a relationship with Jesus. By using Eve's mistake as a warning, we can grow in obedience to God's commands, big and small.

Recall a specific time when you realized you sinned against God. How did you respond?

Day 3

The man said, "This is now bone of my bones and flesh of my flesh; she shall be called 'woman,' for she was taken out of man."
GENESIS 2:23

Eve is someone who has been defined by her mistakes for thousands of years. Literally thousands. Can you imagine? Can you imagine if your worst mistake, the offense you committed that you were *most* ashamed of, echoed through millennia and became one of the single most important moments in redemptive history?

Yikes. We may worry that our biggest mistakes get publicized on social media and go viral. That would be bad enough. But being known as "that girl who started the whole sin thing" for all of written history is infinitely worse. And yet that's not the whole of who Eve was. Remember how we talked about womankind being the missing piece of the creation puzzle? God fitted that perfect piece through Eve. She was *that* before she was "the sin girl."

You are not defined by your mistakes, either, no matter how much it feels that way sometimes. God saw Eve as the complete

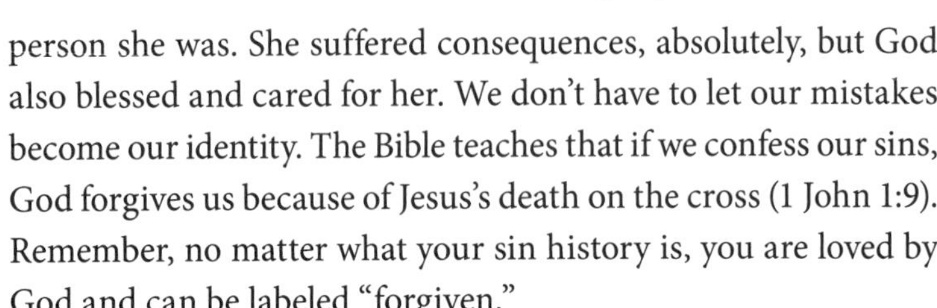

person she was. She suffered consequences, absolutely, but God also blessed and cared for her. We don't have to let our mistakes become our identity. The Bible teaches that if we confess our sins, God forgives us because of Jesus's death on the cross (1 John 1:9). Remember, no matter what your sin history is, you are loved by God and can be labeled "forgiven."

Describe a time when you felt defined by your mistakes. How did you overcome it?

Day 4

"You will not certainly die," the serpent said to the woman. "For God knows that when you eat from it your eyes will be opened, and you will be like God, knowing good and evil."

GENESIS 3:4–5

Oh, Eve. The fateful words of the Serpent live on in infamy, and each time we read them, we may have the desire to shout at her, "Don't do it!" We know the end of the story. We feel the effects of Eve's actions each day as we battle against our own selfish desires.

Even though most of our struggle with obedience to God might come from within, battling our own impulses or wrong choices, we're not unlike Eve. The voice of the Enemy whispers in our ear and wants to derail us.

Perhaps it's someone in your life you know is a negative influence, constantly tugging you away from God. Perhaps it's a worldview which says there is no God, and everywhere you turn, you're confronted by a voice asking you, "Did God *really* say . . ." We can learn from Eve's mistake. We know how it turns

out when we give in to the Enemy. Return to God's Word to reaffirm all you know to be true and battle against those deceptive whispers. The Serpent wants to harm us. But God loves us and his commands are always for our own good.

What life lessons does Eve's story teach you?

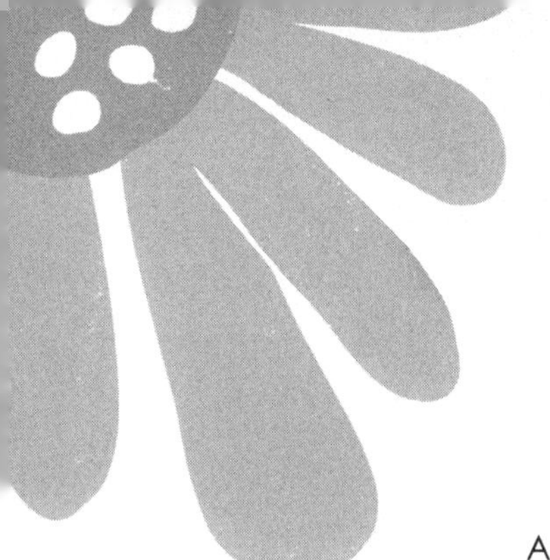

Day 5

And he said, "Who told you that you were naked? Have you eaten from the tree that I commanded you not to eat from?" The man said, "The woman you put here with me—she gave me some fruit from the tree, and I ate it." Then the LORD God said to the woman, "What is this you have done?" The woman said, "The serpent deceived me, and I ate."

GENESIS 3:11–13

It took about three seconds from the time we first sinned to the time we first shifted the blame to someone else. And let's be real—that struggle continues today in full force. Small children don't need to be taught to try to blame someone else for their wrongdoing. We have a natural, if sinful, instinct to try to wriggle out of trouble.

But accepting blame when we've messed up is important. Really important. It goes so much deeper than just being willing to face our consequences or making sure someone else doesn't have to face the repercussions of our actions. These things matter, of course, but they matter in a worldly sense.

Accepting responsibility is *spiritually* important because it's the first step toward repentance. If we're busy trying to convince others (or ourselves) that we did nothing wrong—that the Serpent made us do it—then we can't turn away from that wrongdoing. We can't apologize to God or anyone else we've hurt. We can't walk away from that mistake and commit to never do it again. Accepting responsibility is the start; true repentance is the goal.

Why is taking responsibility when you mess up a better choice than blaming someone else?

Accepting responsibility is spiritually important because it's the first step toward repentance.

Day 6

He took his wife Sarai, his nephew Lot, all the possessions they had accumulated and the people they had acquired in Harran, and they set out for the land of Canaan, and they arrived there.

GENESIS 12:5

If Abraham is the father of God's people, then Sarah must be our mother. Of course, when we first meet Sarah in Genesis 12, she's called Sarai and Abraham is still Abram. God is just beginning to intersect with their lives in a very dynamic, special way.

And that's really what Abraham and Sarah's story is all about—the wild, divine intersection of God and his human creations. God makes this couple promises that seem unbelievable—then he follows through. God directs them to move several times. God changes both their names. He blesses them, speaks with them, meets with them. In Abraham, we see one of the clearest examples of God taking a faithful person by the hand and guiding his steps.

And Sarah was a part of it all, sometimes displaying the same sort of faith her husband is remembered for, and other times

showing us examples of how *not* to respond to our major life events. Sarah is real and human, and we can learn a lot from reading her story.

What are some of the biggest choices you've made so far? What have you learned?

Day 7

Now Sarai, Abram's wife, had
borne him no children. But she
had an Egyptian slave named Hagar.
GENESIS 16:1

Each of our stories is intertwined with the stories of many other people. Our parents, our siblings, our friends, our neighbors, our coworkers. At some points, our stories become so deeply connected with others', it's impossible to tell one story without telling the other. That's how it is with Sarai and Hagar.

It's hard to say how we should classify Sarai and Hagar's relationship. Hagar was Sarai's maidservant. But were they strictly employer-employee? Or were they personally close, like friends? Maybe they were even like sisters, sharing living space the way they did. We only get glimpses of their personal relationship, and it's after trouble strikes. Major friction ensues.

There are so many bits of wisdom to glean from the stories of these two ladies, but it's difficult to avoid feeling sorry about their interpersonal problems. Think of all the wonderful women in your life—your mom, sisters, female friends, mentors, teachers, or neighbors. Thank God for blessing you with the wonderful women whose stories intertwine with yours.

Who are the girls and women you are most connected to? How do these connections make your life better?

Day 8

[Sarai] said to Abram, "The LORD has kept me from having children. Go, sleep with my slave; perhaps I can build a family through her." Abram agreed to what Sarai said.

GENESIS 16:2

Now, I know what you're thinking. If we judge Sarai by today's standards, she sounds absolutely crazy. Any modern wife would be incredibly upset if her husband had a sexual relationship with another woman—and rightly so! But Sarai was acting in accordance with the custom of her time. A male heir was considered absolutely vital, and Sarai had grown tired of waiting for the heir God had promised to her husband.

Before we judge Sarai too harshly, we should recognize that we don't know how much time passed between Genesis 15 when Abram received the promise of an heir and Genesis 16 when Sarai hands Hagar over to Abram. Perhaps Sarai was well past childbearing years already and thought she *must* fall in line with this ancient custom to make God's words come true. Whatever her motivation, her actions had pretty serious consequences for all involved.

Taking matters into our own hands to this degree rarely produces good results. It's good to be proactive, but we need to balance our initiative with the trust that when God says he'll do something—he will accomplish those things.

Have you ever made an impulsive decision you later regretted? If so, what did you learn?

Day 9

And [Hagar] conceived. When she knew she was pregnant, she began to despise her mistress. Then Sarai said to Abram, "You are responsible for the wrong I am suffering. I put my slave in your arms, and now that she knows she is pregnant, she despises me. May the Lord judge between you and me."

GENESIS 16:4–5

Hagar fell into a trap we all do sometimes. When she saw that she was able to do something her mistress wasn't able to do—in this case, give Abram a child—she became haughty. Arrogant. Conceited. She was so puffed up about it, she despised her mistress, the woman whom she had lived with for some time.

Overinflated egos can be big relationship killers. No one wants to be close with the girl who thinks she's better than everyone else. It's important that we speak positively about ourselves and recognize that we are loved and beautiful, strong and capable in Christ. When we begin to feel superior, we've crossed a line that could spell doom for our most treasured friendships.

It's sad when relationships fall apart, especially when they

fall apart because of our wrong attitudes. Is there someone you were once close with, but now you've drifted apart? Pray about what you can do to help set things right, especially if the distance was caused by a mistake you made. Relationships can be healed when we're willing to humble ourselves!

How would you describe the difference between self-confidence and an overinflated ego?

Day 10

And [the angel of the Lord] said, "Hagar, slave of Sarai, where have you come from, and where are you going?" "I'm running away from my mistress Sarai," she answered.
GENESIS 16:8

Everyone messes up. We make bad choices, adopt wrong attitudes, hurt other people. We wish we didn't do these things most of the time, especially when the heat of the moment has passed and we're confronted with the fallout of our actions. Repercussions—bleh. Consequences—ick.

No matter how hard it is to face the music, running away from our consequences is never the best choice. It's the easiest choice, certainly. And sometimes it feels like our only option. When we've tripped up big-time and it feels like there's no way back, running away seems like the logical thing to do.

But God doesn't work this way. The Bible says that when we plant bad choices, we will harvest consequences (it's the "reaping and sowing" principle). This feels like a hard truth. And it is. But through these hard experiences where we must swallow our pride and put aside our fears, we grow. This spiritual growth may

not undo whatever mistake we made. But through that growth, we move one step closer to maturity, toward a spirit that looks more and more like Jesus's. It's hard and it hurts. But it's always worth it.

Think about a time when you had to face consequences for a bad choice. Did the consequences deter you from making the same mistake again? Why or why not?

Day 11

[Hagar] gave this name to the LORD who spoke to her: "You are the God who sees me," for she said, "I have now seen the One who sees me."
GENESIS 16:13

Have you ever felt misunderstood, like no one gets you? Or maybe like no matter how hard you try to relate to others, you're just on a different wavelength than everyone else? It would probably be too ironic if I told you, "You're not alone." But it's true. Many people feel that same sting of loneliness. Some feel it more often than others, but everyone has probably experienced it at one point or another.

Did you know that we have a God who sees us? And not just in the sense that we see an object or person in front of us and can discern its appearance. Our God *sees* us—our whole selves, from our outer appearance, to our inner organs, to our minds and hearts. Our very souls are not only seen but *understood* by God.

If you ever feel alone and lost like Hagar was, remember that there is a God who sees you and everything you're going through. He is there to talk to, to comfort you, and to lead you toward your next step. You never need to feel like no one gets you. God does.

It's an exciting thing when we meet a friend who "gets us." How does it impact you when you think about the reality that God "gets you" and understands you completely?

Day 12

God also said to Abraham, "As for Sarai your wife, you are no longer to call her Sarai; her name will be Sarah. I will bless her and will surely give you a son by her. I will bless her so that she will be the mother of nations; kings of peoples will come from her."

GENESIS 17:15–16

Sarai had her name for many decades. She was probably pretty comfortable with it. And then God decreed that her name would be Sarah instead of Sarai. Why? Sarai means "my princess" in Hebrew. Sarah is a similar name with the same root, but it has grander connotations—almost like "Queen Mother" or "mother of nations." A fitting change for the role God was asking Sarai to assume.

We don't usually change our actual names, but our relationship with God does change our labels, and that's really what God was doing here for Sarai. Can you think of a few labels you ascribed to yourself before God began to change you into Christ's image?

Maybe you used to feel like a screw-up—like nothing you

did was right—but now God has removed that label and shown you how loved you are. Or maybe you felt like everything you did was perfect, but now God has removed that label and replaced it with humility to show you places you need to grow. What other labels might God want to replace for you so you can better fulfill his purpose in your life?

What new, positive labels do you have because of your relationship with God?

Day 13

Then one of them said, "I will surely return to you about this time next year, and Sarah your wife will have a son." Now Sarah was listening at the entrance to the tent, which was behind him. Abraham and Sarah were already very old, and Sarah was past the age of childbearing. So Sarah laughed to herself as she thought, "After I am worn out and my lord is old, will I now have this pleasure?"

GENESIS 18:10–12

Sarah received the mother of all promises (bad pun intended). God promised Sarah a pregnancy when she was old enough to be a great-grandmother. I'm sure she would have loved to hear these words decades earlier. But now? When she's very old and has given up on the idea of producing Abraham's heir? That must have been a pretty difficult promise to believe. And indeed, Sarah laughed when she heard it. Who can blame her?

Sometimes we're asked to believe in the impossible. Really, the foundation of our faith can seem "impossible"—the God of the universe born as a man and dying on a cross for our sins.

Impossible, yet true. It's important that we build up our belief muscle—the one that flexes and says, "God can do all things, even if we don't understand how." That's faith.

God certainly followed through for Sarah. In Genesis 21, we read that she became pregnant and gave birth to a son, just at the time God promised she would. When God promises us something, he won't go back on it. He always follows through, no matter how impossible his promises may seem.

Which promises in Scripture are you waiting on God to fulfill in your life?

Day 14

Before he had finished praying, Rebekah came out with her jar on her shoulder. She was the daughter of Bethuel son of Milkah, who was the wife of Abraham's brother Nahor.
GENESIS 24:15

We know Isaac was a special kid, the fulfillment of a promise given to Abraham and Sarah, who were far too old to have biological children. And of course, Isaac eventually grew up and got married himself. Rebekah was his wife, and they have a legitimate love story. Arranged marriage was the common custom in those days, and Isaac and Rebekah's marriage *was* arranged—they'd never even met when she agreed to be his wife! But Isaac romantically loved Rebekah, too, which sets them apart.

This doesn't mean their relationship was without bumps. In fact, from Rebekah, we see a spectrum of wonderful and troubling qualities. Like Sarah before her, Rebekah is shown to be a real, flawed, three-dimensional person. Someone we can relate to and learn from, and someone whose story helps us to grow in godliness.

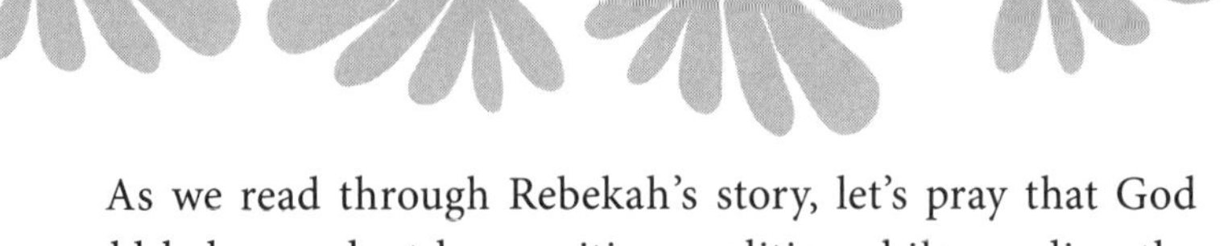

As we read through Rebekah's story, let's pray that God would help us adopt her positive qualities while weeding the negative ones from our hearts.

Do you think good people can have both wonderful and troubling qualities? What can you learn from both?

Day 15

I want you to swear by the Lord, the God of heaven and the God of earth, that you will not get a wife for my son from the daughters of the Canaanites, among whom I am living, but will go to my country and my own relatives and get a wife for my son Isaac.

GENESIS 24:3–4

The long journey that brought Abraham's servant to Rebekah's front door began here. Abraham's servant was instructed by Abraham to return to Abraham's homeland and find a wife for his son, Isaac. These days, it might sound weird for a dad to request that his son's wife come from his relatives. But in Isaac's time, it was perfectly normal to marry within one's clan—and keep in mind, Abraham's family had grown!

Today, we obviously like a wider gene pool in our marriages, but we can still draw a valuable lesson from Abraham's request. Abraham wanted to find a partner for Isaac who would share his values and understand his faith. The same idea is important for us when we are thinking about dating or even friendships.

This doesn't mean we have to *only* hang out with people who

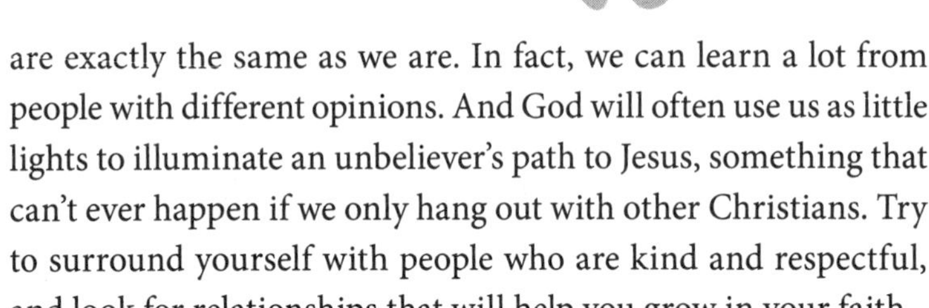

are exactly the same as we are. In fact, we can learn a lot from people with different opinions. And God will often use us as little lights to illuminate an unbeliever's path to Jesus, something that can't ever happen if we only hang out with other Christians. Try to surround yourself with people who are kind and respectful, and look for relationships that will help you grow in your faith.

Who are the people that help you grow in your faith?

Day 16

Then they said, "Let's call the young woman and ask her about it." So they called Rebekah and asked her, "Will you go with this man?" "I will go," she said.
GENESIS 24:57–58

People generally like to be comfortable. Many of us like routine, familiarity, and safety. Even the free-spirited, spontaneous among us tend to have a comfort zone—somewhere they return to after their exciting adventures in the big, wide world.

But God asks us to step outside of our comfort zones on a daily basis. By loving him and serving him with our lives, we're already in a culturally uncomfortable place. Other people may not understand our faith, and they may dislike or ridicule us because of it. When we're being asked to go to the uncomfortable, unknown places in life, are we willing? Like Rebekah, will we say, "I will go"?

Are there any areas in your life right now where God is asking you to get uncomfortable? Where does God want to grow you or stretch you? Take a few minutes to pray about it. Ask God for the bravery to say, "I will go" when he asks!

In what ways has God nudged you out of your comfort zone?

Day 17

The boys grew up, and Esau became a skillful hunter, a man of the open country, while Jacob was content to stay at home among the tents. Isaac, who had a taste for wild game, loved Esau, but Rebekah loved Jacob.

GENESIS 25:27–28

Since God was building a nation, it shouldn't surprise us that Isaac and Rebekah had children—twin sons, Esau and Jacob. The boys' relationship started off rocky. As the oldest son, Esau would have inherited twice as much wealth as his brother. It would make sense to assume Esau was the son through whom God would continue to fulfill his promise to Abraham.

But God had other plans. Jacob was chosen as the son of promise. Already there was fertile ground for some serious sibling rivalry. But here we read that, on top of everything else, Isaac and Rebekah played favorites with their boys. Ouch.

Have you ever felt like you're on the wrong side of the favoritism game? Like you've been overlooked or that you don't measure up when compared to someone else? Maybe it's with a parent, but

it could also be with a teacher, coach, or even in your group of friends. Favoritism stings, and it never breeds healthy relationships. But we have to remember that we have no control over how others feel about or view us. We can choose to let go of our resentment and be sure we don't fall into the favoritism trap ourselves.

What is a healthy way to respond when you are overlooked?

Day 18

Rebekah said to her son Jacob, "Look, I overheard your father say to your brother Esau, 'Bring me some game and prepare me some tasty food to eat, so that I may give you my blessing in the presence of the LORD before I die.' Now, my son, listen carefully and do what I tell you: Go out to the flock and bring me two choice young goats, so I can prepare some tasty food for your father, just the way he likes it. Then take it to your father to eat, so that he may give you his blessing before he dies."

GENESIS 27:6–10

Oh, Rebekah. She concocted quite the plan here to make sure her favorite son, Jacob, was blessed beyond her husband's favorite, Esau. Esau, as the oldest, was to receive a double inheritance (he ended up selling it to Jacob for a bowl of soup—not a good life choice). Perhaps Rebekah felt like Jacob's position was not secure and her favored boy would get left in the dust.

So, what was so bad about her plan? Aside from the obvious—Rebekah failed to recognize that God had already promised Jacob would be the father of the nation of Israel. It was pronounced long before this trick. Like Sarah, Rebekah seemed to want to take matters into her own hands to force God's promise to come true.

God doesn't need our help to keep his promises. He doesn't need anything from us at all. What he *wants* is our trust and our obedience. When we honor God with our trust in his words, he is glorified all the more when he stays true to his promises.

What are you trusting God for right now?

Day 19

Then Rebekah said to Isaac, "I'm disgusted with living because of these Hittite women. If Jacob takes a wife from among the women of this land, from Hittite women like these, my life will not be worth living."

GENESIS 27:46

Rebekah may have been acting a little dramatic about her daughters-in-law here. Yes, there were very sharp religious differences between Isaac's family and the surrounding people groups who worshiped idols. Perhaps the difference in values between Rebekah's family and the wives her son Esau had taken really made Rebekah's life miserable.

One thing is certain—we generally don't want a family member to feel upset or uncomfortable because of us in the way Rebekah was upset by Esau's wives. We don't want to be known as a bringer of grief (or drama or bad attitude). This idea can even be applied to our friends and other people close to us, whether by birth, marriage, or choice. Instead, we want to be known as someone who brings blessing with her presence.

What can you do today to bless those around you?

Day 20

While he was still talking with them, Rachel came with her father's sheep, for she was a shepherd. When Jacob saw Rachel daughter of his uncle Laban, and Laban's sheep, he went over and rolled the stone away from the mouth of the well and watered his uncle's sheep.

GENESIS 29:9–10

There aren't many women in the Bible who are given as much room on the stage as Rachel. We get to know a lot about this woman who eventually becomes the beloved wife of Jacob. And that means we get to see the good, the bad, and the ugly. Perhaps this is what makes Rachel (and her sister, whom we'll meet soon) so relatable.

Rachel would eventually become Jacob's wife, but before that, she had a job. We might get the idea that ancient women were chained to their ovens and looms, but they actually shared in a surprising number of duties we tend to associate with men, like tending the flocks and herds. Rachel was a shepherdess. And in biblical days, the animals Rachel tended were highly valuable—a family's wealth could be measured by the quantity and quality of its flocks and herds.

Today, let's thank God that, as modern women, we have choices about how we'd like to spend our lives, both personally and professionally. Not every generation of women before us has enjoyed such freedom. It's a blessing!

Do you sense God guiding you to a specific type of work? If so, what is it?

Day 21

Leah had weak eyes, but Rachel had a lovely figure and was beautiful.
GENESIS 29:17

Weak eyes? It almost seems like we have a strange, biblical comment on Leah's eyesight—that she would be a candidate for LASIK. Or at least glasses (join the club). But the Hebrew phrase for "weak eyes" can mean gentle, kind eyes. Or it can be an insult, suggesting Leah's eyes weren't exactly stunning. And given what follows about Rachel, that may very well be what the original writer meant.

Rachel was "the pretty sister." Ugh. Comparisons like this can be so painful. If you have a sister, cousin, or close female friend to whom you're often compared, you know how this feels. The pretty sister. The smart one. The athletic one. The artsy or musical one. Or how about "the good one"? Ouch.

Whenever we feel like we're compared to someone else and found wanting, it can hurt. But we don't have to own the negative comparisons others foist upon us. We can choose to focus on our strengths, the wonderful things that God and others see when they look at us. We *all* have these qualities, and yet we're so prone

to embracing the negative descriptors instead. Think about your positives today. Focus on embracing those great attributes.

God has gifted you in a variety of ways. What do you see as your greatest strengths?

Day 22

Jacob was in love with Rachel
and said, "I'll work for you seven
years in return for your younger daughter
Rachel." . . . So Jacob served seven years to
get Rachel, but they seemed like only a few
days to him because of his love for her.
GENESIS 29:18, 20

Whoa, buddy! So quick with the marriage talk! It seems a little abrupt as we read through the story in Genesis. Jacob and Rachel seem to fall in love immediately and jump straight into discussions of marriage arrangements. But when you think about it, marriage *talk* happened quickly. The actual marriage was planned for seven years away. And even by today's standards, that's a very long engagement. The idea of "true love" can sometimes tie us up in knots. We may watch romantic comedies and think those "love stories" are what true love looks like—the flutteriest butterflies, the most sparks, the biggest romantic gestures. Or we may think it's common (or even possible) to meet a man and know instantly he's our soulmate. (Yikes—let's avoid that territory, ladies.)

But Jacob would probably tell us true love looks a lot like hard work. He labored for *seven years* before he was able to possibly marry Rachel. All relationships that really matter require time and effort. But they're worth it!

In what ways do relationships require a lot of hard work?

Day 23

But when evening came, he took his daughter Leah and brought her to Jacob . . . When morning came, there was Leah! So Jacob said to Laban, "What is this you have done to me? I served you for Rachel, didn't I? Why have you deceived me?"

GENESIS 29:23, 25

The word "leftovers" doesn't bring to mind the prettiest picture. We might think of two-day-old food, stale and soggy, sealed in a plastic container and waiting for some very hungry person with no other options to consider heating it up and braving a bite. Is that what Leah felt like here—the leftover sister?

It's not that Jacob didn't have a right to be angry. He and Laban had an agreement. He was to work for seven long years—which he did—and then receive *Rachel* as his wife. And remember how much he loved Rachel. Instead, Laban tricked him into marrying Leah. Jacob had every right to be upset. But . . . what about Leah?

We don't get a biblical comment on how Leah felt in this moment, but we can imagine she knew exactly how much she was *not* Jacob's first choice. In fact, she would spend much of the

rest of her life trying to win his attention. It must have felt like being picked last for a sports team—times a million.

But no matter how others see us, God sees us as his beloved, not his last choice. We're precious, not picked-over.

Why is it important to be convinced that God loves and cherishes you?

Day 24

[Laban said], "Finish this daughter's bridal week; then we will give you the younger one also, in return for another seven years of work."
GENESIS 29:27

The good news for Rachel was, after seven long years, she only had to wait another week before marrying Jacob. The less-good news was that her older sister was now also married to the guy she loved. Awkward.

Even more awkward . . . do you notice how Laban speaks of Rachel here? "The younger one." He doesn't mention her by name. And he tacks her on to the deal like an afterthought: "Yeah, we'll give her to you too." How did Rachel feel about that? We can guess she was pretty accustomed to being the favored sister, but suddenly, she becomes the unnamed afterthought.

Have you ever been toppled like that? It's amazing how quickly things can flip. Our positions are never secure. One second, we're on the top of the social food chain, and the next, we've plummeted to the bottom. If we look to our social standing to tell us what we're worth, we're putting our trust in a very

shaky system! Instead, we can plant our sense of self-worth very securely on God. *He* says we're beloved, and we are—no matter what others think of us.

Why is it dangerous to place our worth on our social standing?

If we look to our social standing to tell us what we're worth, we're putting our trust in a very shaky system! Instead, we can plant our self-worth very securely on God.

Day 25

When Rachel saw that she was not bearing Jacob any children, she became jealous of her sister. So she said to Jacob, "Give me children, or I'll die!"

GENESIS 30:1

As the favored wife, Rachel didn't have much reason to be jealous of Leah—at first. But by this time, the unloved Leah had been blessed (and blessed Jacob) with four sons. Four of them! The first three times Leah gave birth to a son, she said something to the effect of "*Now* my husband will surely love me!" These sons didn't seem to affect the way Jacob felt about Leah, but they did cause some strong feelings in Rachel.

Learning to manage our jealousy is very important. Envy is the sort of thing that can begin as a tiny seed. If we allow that tiny seed to grow some roots and sprout a few leaves, we'll have a tree of jealousy on our hands before we know it. And those trees are destructive. They cause relationships to crumble, sometimes beyond repair. In Rachel and Leah's case, the jealousy between these two sisters began an escalating race to bear Jacob the most children. The echoes of this rivalry carried into the next generation.

Take a moment to think about any jealousy seeds in your life that are trying to sprout. Dig those things out before they put down roots!

Pray and ask God to help you deal with jealousy. What other practical steps can you take to deal with jealousy?

Day 26

[Rachel] became pregnant and
gave birth to a son and said,
"God has taken away my disgrace."
She named him Joseph, and said, "May
the Lord add to me another son."
GENESIS 30:23–24

As modern women who aren't judged "worthy" based on the number of sons we have, we may want to tell Rachel she wasn't a disgrace, even without children of her own (and we'd be right!). But it's not really the point here. For Rachel, baby Joseph was a sweet answer to many years of longing for a child. We can only imagine how often Rachel prayed, cried, and hurt over the baby who never seemed to come.

Do you have a close-held dream in your heart? Maybe it has to do with your education or career. Maybe it has to do with being a wife or mother. Maybe it has to do with places you want to see or people you want to meet. Most of us have dreams in at least one of these categories. And the scary truth is, we're not promised that all our dreams will come true. What we *are* promised is God knows exactly what we need, when we need it.

When we place our dreams and desires in his hands, trusting that he knows what he's doing, we can have peace that our lives are unfolding just the way *he* wants them to.

What dreams do you hold closest to your heart?

Day 27

Then Rachel and Leah replied [to Jacob], "Do we still have any share in the inheritance of our father's estate? Does he not regard us as foreigners? Not only has he sold us, but he has used up what was paid for us. Surely all the wealth that God took away from our father belongs to us and our children. So do whatever God has told you."

GENESIS 31:14–16

It's sad that this is the way Leah and Rachel ended up leaving their father's land. But we can hardly blame them. Their father used them as pawns in his marriage schemes with Jacob. He had used their husband to try to increase his own wealth. Laban did not treat Leah and Rachel as beloved daughters. He treated them like game pieces.

It never feels good when someone uses us for selfish reasons. But it hurts even more when the person using us is someone who is supposed to love and cherish us. How do we respond? How do we deal with that?

The answer varies case by case. Sometimes, gentle confrontation is necessary. Other times, overlooking personal slights

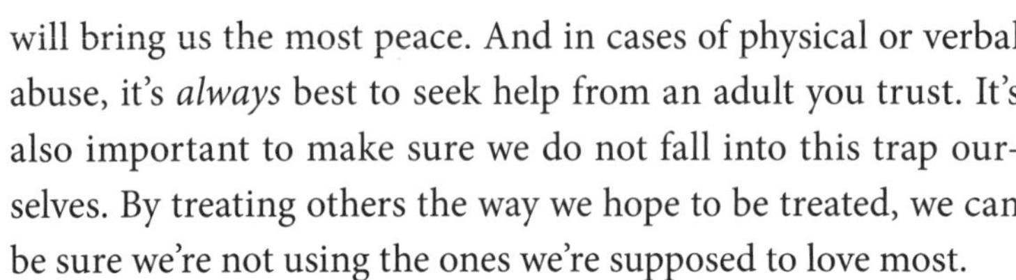

will bring us the most peace. And in cases of physical or verbal abuse, it's *always* best to seek help from an adult you trust. It's also important to make sure we do not fall into this trap ourselves. By treating others the way we hope to be treated, we can be sure we're not using the ones we're supposed to love most.

Make a short list of things you value in a relationship. How do you prefer to be treated? Are you treating other people the way you prefer to be treated? If not, what steps can you take to improve?

Day 28

There Abraham and his wife Sarah were buried, there Isaac and his wife Rebekah were buried, and there I buried Leah.
GENESIS 49:31

It's an interesting final twist in Leah's story. She was not the favored wife in life, but in death, she was buried in the family plot while the beloved Rachel was buried by the side of the road. But, while Leah had this final bit of honor in death, her disappointment in life was known by all. Is it any surprise, then, that the rivalry between Leah and Rachel carried on into the next generation? Rachel's oldest son, Joseph, was favored by his father and despised by his half-brothers, Leah's sons.

It's easy to take on the offenses of others, especially when family honor is at stake. But Jesus teaches a very different method of dealing with offenses against us. In Luke 17, he tells us to rebuke brothers and sisters who sin against us, certainly, but then to forgive freely. Paul repeated this teaching in his letters to various churches.

Forgiveness is *hard*. Family feuds are one thing, but even a simple disagreement between two friends can be difficult to

reconcile. But when we bring Jesus's spirit of openness (in frankly discussing the offense) and forgiveness (showing the grace to others that's been shown to us), reconciliation *is* possible.

Describe a time when you struggled to forgive someone. How did you overcome it?

Day 29

Then Miriam the prophet, Aaron's sister, took a timbrel in her hand, and all the women followed her, with timbrels and dancing.

EXODUS 15:20

We've fast-forwarded a bit into the book of Exodus, where we'll meet Moses's sister, Miriam. "Miriam the prophet." It's a brief mention, but it's kind of a big deal. We don't have a huge number of female prophets discussed in the Bible (though there are more than many people realize!). Not only is Miriam called a prophet, she is leading all the women of Israel in a song and dance. Prophet and musician—basically, Miriam was an ancient girl boss.

We're pretty lucky to be born in the era we are. Never before has such a large percentage of the global female population had as much freedom as we enjoy. We have the opportunity to pursue careers, rock out being a stay-at-home wife or mom, stay single and support ourselves, shoot for the very highest levels of education available, compete in professional sports—just about anything we want!

But not all girls around the globe have these opportunities. Women in other cultures often deal with constant threats to

their safety, little or no freedom, and barbaric practices left over from centuries past. Remember to pray for these women. There are Christian organizations that specifically offer help to these women and their children. See what you can do to get involved!

There are many women around the world who are vulnerable and lack opportunities. Which groups are closest to your heart?

Day 30

Miriam and Aaron began to talk against Moses because of his Cushite wife, for he had married a Cushite.

NUMBERS 12:1

This is a sad piece of the story. Miriam and Aaron are (wrongly, as we'll see later) speaking out against their own brother. But perhaps even more importantly, they are speaking out against the leader God had anointed. They may have even thought they were doing the right thing, since Moses had married a foreign woman and God generally wanted the Israelites to marry other Israelites so they wouldn't be drawn into the idol worship of the cultures around them. But they did not seek God on the matter before speaking out against their brother. Instead, they slandered him.

Now, this is very important to understand. Aaron and Miriam were sinning because they were *slandering* Moses—that is, they were accusing this godly man of sinning when he hadn't. This is not the same thing as speaking out against someone in authority who is being abusive.

But we must be very careful when we consider speaking against our Christian leaders—and people, in general. Before

saying anything negative or critical, make sure you are speaking the truth from a place of love, and that your motivations are good (and not rooted in jealousy, like Miriam and Aaron's).

What is the difference between speaking critically or slandering someone and speaking out when someone is being abusive?

Day 31

At once the LORD said to Moses, Aaron and Miriam, "Come out to the tent of meeting, all three of you." So the three of them went out. Then the LORD came down in a pillar of cloud; he stood at the entrance to the tent and summoned Aaron and Miriam.

NUMBERS 12:4–5

Gulp. This would be like being called to the principal's office times a million. God had some choice words for Aaron and Miriam because they had been unjust in accusing Moses. And God told them that Moses was special, even among his prophets. In other words, "Back off, Miriam and Aaron!"

Part of maturing is learning to accept discipline when we've earned it. And, man, do we earn it sometimes. No matter how hard we try, we all mess up. We all make mistakes. Accepting correction from those in authority over us is an important part of learning from those mistakes. That person in authority may be a teacher or boss, and very often this correction comes from our parents. It may even come from our friends. We are wise to listen to the correction of those who love us—friends, family,

and mentors or pastors we're close to. It's not an easy aspect of maturing, but it's an important one!

Miriam and Aaron were guilty of speaking unjustly about Moses. Why is it so important to be careful with words?

Day 32

The anger of the LORD burned against them, and he left them. When the cloud lifted from above the tent, Miriam's skin was leprous—it became as white as snow. Aaron turned toward her and saw that she had a defiling skin disease, and he said to Moses, 'Please, my lord, I ask you not to hold against us the sin we have so foolishly committed. Do not let her be like a stillborn infant coming from its mother's womb with its flesh half eaten away.'

NUMBERS 12:9–12

Leprosy was no joke in the ancient world. Miriam was experiencing some pretty serious consequences for her accusations against her brother.

Aaron quickly recognizes he and Miriam had acted foolishly and he speaks up on his sister's behalf. And God did actually heal Miriam in this case. But worldly consequences don't often work that way. When we mess up and experience consequences, those consequences tend to stick around. Even if we're sorry.

The best way to avoid worldly consequences is to avoid the

mess-ups in the first place. Obviously. Remembering that consequences can be long-lasting can serve as a good motivator for thinking twice about our words and actions. But when we do stumble, we can and should pray to God for mercy. But the correction we experience through consequences will result in growth and—hopefully—wiser choices in the future.

Which consequences motivate you to avoid specific behavior?

Remembering that consequences can be long-lasting can serve as a good motivator for thinking twice about our words and actions. But when we do stumble, we can and should pray to God for mercy.

Day 33

So Moses cried out to the Lord,
"Please, God, heal her!"
NUMBERS 12:13

This is a short verse, but it contains a very powerful message. Miriam and Aaron have wrongly accused their little brother Moses. Even God took Moses's side and punished Miriam for her arrogance. But instead of leaving Miriam to the consequences she earned, as would be very tempting to do, Moses cries out to God for her. He asks for her healing. He asks God's grace for Miriam, even though she messed up. Even though her mess-up was specifically against Moses.

That's forgiveness. It isn't always easy to read Jesus's teachings about forgiveness in the New Testament. He sets a really high standard for us, and forgiveness can be one of the most difficult things for many people to practice. So it's a good thing we have people—regular human beings, just like us—who displayed this trait well in the Bible.

Have you been wronged before? Most of us have. Have you been able to forgive the friend who wronged you? God can soften our hearts and make it possible if we let him.

Is it harder for you to forgive someone else or yourself?

Day 34

> I brought you up out of Egypt and redeemed you from the land of slavery. I sent Moses to lead you, also Aaron and Miriam.
>
> **MICAH 6:4**

Miriam wasn't as perfect as the rest of us (ahem . . .). She was a woman who had an up-and-down journey. An honored leader and prophet. A woman who let her arrogance cloud her judgment. A woman who was publicly disciplined. An artist immortalized in song. Miriam was all of these things, and more.

But here in the book of Micah, hundreds of years after Miriam lived and God saved his people from Egypt, God once again honors Miriam by referring to her not as a person who made mistakes, but as a woman who he sent, along with her brothers, to save his people from Egypt. It's a powerful redemption for our complex Miriam. Her story didn't end with "she made a huge mistake and God was angry with her."

Our stories are always in progress. Sometimes, when difficult things happen in our lives, it can feel like this is our whole story, now and forevermore. Maybe we worry that our stories are over. But God is always writing a new chapter. When we can't see the whole book, God nudges us to at least flip the page.

Have you ever made such a serious mistake that you felt your life was over? How is God continuing to write your story?

Day 35

Then Joshua son of Nun secretly sent two spies from Shittim. "Go, look over the land," he said, "especially Jericho." So they went and entered the house of a prostitute named Rahab and stayed there.

JOSHUA 2:1

It's a pretty humble one, as "first mentions" go. She's not Rahab, the business owner, or Rahab, the homeowner, or even just Rahab. She is Rahab, the Canaanite prostitute. Probably not the title any of us would want to announce our arrival in the Bible.

But, despite this unflattering first mention, Rahab becomes a legitimate hero of the Bible. In fact, she gets three mentions in the New Testament, so long-lasting was her impact. Here in Joshua, Rahab was writing the very beginning of a new story for herself and her family.

Maybe you're in the same position in your family. Maybe you're the first person in your family to believe in God. Or maybe you're simply feeling young and small, unsure how you'll be able to have a positive impact on the kingdom of God. Don't resent

starting out from humble beginnings. Rahab rose to be a superstar of faith, and you can too.

Why is Rahab a good example of how God can turn any life around?

Day 36

> The king of Jericho was told, "Look, some of the Israelites have come here tonight to spy out the land." So the king of Jericho sent this message to Rahab: "Bring out the men who came to you and entered your house, because they have come to spy out the whole land."
>
> **JOSHUA 2:2–3**

Rahab was risking her safety, and possibly her life, to help the Hebrew strangers. It might make us think of Jesus's words in John 15:13: "Greater love has no one than this: to lay down one's life for one's friends." Those are words of intense bravery.

It runs against our natural instinct (self-preservation) to sacrifice ourselves for others. We may not ever experience a demand for self-sacrifice as dramatic as Rahab did here, although many in the 1940s were faced with a frighteningly similar situation as Jewish refugees fled from Nazis during World War II.

But self-sacrifice happens in quiet ways too. It happens in being an emotional support for a struggling friend, in getting up early on a Saturday to serve your community, in volunteering

time, energy, and material resources to help those in need. It happens in putting others first and showing sacrificial love.

Who is someone who has shown you sacrificial love? What did they do and how did it make you feel?

Day 37

We have heard how the LORD dried up the water of the Red Sea for you when you came out of Egypt, and what you did to Sihon and Og, the two kings of the Amorites east of the Jordan, whom you completely destroyed. When we heard of it, our hearts melted in fear and everyone's courage failed because of you, for the LORD your God is God in heaven above and on the earth below.

JOSHUA 2:10–11

Notice what Rahab says here—*we* have heard. The Israelites' reputation preceded them. The whole city of Jericho had heard the news of the Israelites escaping through the Red Sea. All of Jericho was afraid because perhaps they were next on the list to be steamrolled by this wandering people and their powerful God.

But for all their fear, Rahab was the *only* one who actually responded to God in her heart. Response is so important. We can hear the gospel message a million and one times but if we don't respond with faith, it's all for nothing.

This matters in our spiritual lives, and it matters in our daily

lives too. Think about some opportunities you might be holding back on. Have you been wanting to try out for a team at school, but you're scared you won't make it? Pray about whether or not God wants you to respond to these opportunities and see where he leads you. He may be nudging you to step out in faith!

What types of fears typically prevent you from stepping out in faith?

Day 38

Now then, please swear to me by the LORD that you will show kindness to my family, because I have shown kindness to you. Give me a sure sign that you will spare the lives of my father and mother, my brothers and sisters, and all who belong to them—and that you will save us from death.

JOSHUA 2:12–13

This is the deal that changed Rahab's life. It was more than just a plea to save her life. If the Israelites pulled off the conquering of Jericho, Rahab's family would be the only family spared from the city. They would be joining a new community—the Israelites—and grafting their Canaanite branch into this nomadic nation.

Did Rahab worry about how smoothly the transition would go? Did she wonder if the Israelites would accept her, the Canaanite prostitute, when the law repeatedly warned the Israelites about intermixing with the Canaanite culture? We can imagine she did. And though we'll never deal with this exact situation, perhaps if we've ever been a stranger crossing the threshold of a new church or school for the first time, we can relate a little bit to how she might have felt.

Sometimes when we're a long-term, comfortable member of a group, it's easy to miss it when someone else is experiencing one of these scary moments of being the newbie or outsider. The next time you see someone new, go the extra mile to welcome them to your community.

What can you do to make newcomers welcome in your circle of friends?

Day 39

But Joshua spared Rahab the prostitute, with her family and all who belonged to her, because she hid the men Joshua had sent as spies to Jericho—and she lives among the Israelites to this day.
JOSHUA 6:25

When we read through the Old Testament, it's pretty clear to see that God chose Israel as his special people. Though he loves everyone, Israel was his promised people. It's important to understand that in order to realize how cool it is that Rahab, a prostitute who was not a born Israelite, was made a member of God's chosen community.

Even many centuries before Jesus came to Earth, God was already hinting at his master plan—a church made up of people of faith, regardless of their heritage. God looked past Rahab's imperfections and into her heart, which held a spark of faith for the one true God. It didn't matter that she didn't have the "qualifications" to be an Israelite.

Your heart is what matters most to God too. We may get discouraged if we feel like we don't have the right upbringing or

the best choices in our past. But none of those things matter to God when we have true faith. God loves you right now, just as you are. While we should always pursue a deeper, better, truer relationship with God, we are beloved even when we are starting out where Rahab did.

In this season of your life, how would you describe your heart toward God?

Day 40

By faith the prostitute Rahab, because she welcomed the spies, was not killed with those who were disobedient.

HEBREWS 11:31

Not only was Rahab honored as a part of Jesus's lineage, she is mentioned here in Hebrews 11, the "Heroes of Faith" chapter. But . . . do you notice something sad? Even here, where she's being honored for her faith and strength of character, she's still called "the prostitute Rahab."

Some sins are "sticky" like that. Even though Rahab was respected, she never could quite shake the label of her past profession. Sometimes it works that way for us too. Sometimes, when people know about the mistakes we've made or the things we used to struggle with, it's hard for them to view us apart from that.

But do you want some good news? God doesn't have this problem. While he is omniscient and knows everything, Psalm 103:12 tells us that as far as the east is from the west, so far has he removed our sins from us. When we repent and accept forgiveness through Jesus, our sin is wiped away, as far as God is

concerned. Humans may not be so perfect in their forgiveness or judgment. But God's truth is the one that really matters. No sin is too sticky for him to remove it from his memory.

Just for a moment think about that sin you'd most like to forget. How does it impact you knowing that Jesus has wiped that sin away and your slate is clean?

Day 41

Now Deborah, a prophet, the wife of Lappidoth, was leading Israel at that time.
JUDGES 4:4

You'd think that after the Israelites entered the promised land, everything would be peachy. But instead (because they were human), they entered into a cycle of falling away from God and his law, being handed over to their enemies, crying out to God, and God sending a deliverer to rescue and lead them. These deliverers were called judges, and Deborah was one of them.

Say what? A female judge of Israel? It's true. Of the fifteen judges mentioned in the Bible, Deborah is the only woman. Was it hard for her to fit in among other Israelite women of her time? Maybe. They were running households and businesses, caring for livestock and fields—no small tasks—but Deborah was leading the nation.

Sometimes being the "only" of something feels like a negative. It can be lonely—the only girl on your debate team, the only girl powerlifting at the gym—or the only Christian girl in the room. But being the "only" one means you're forging a path for

others to follow in the future. "Only" means you're brave enough to do something outside the norm. Like Deborah, your "only" can signal your strength.

Have you experienced being an "only" something? If so, what did you learn?

Day 42

She held court under the Palm of Deborah between Ramah and Bethel in the hill country of Ephraim, and the Israelites went up to her to have their disputes decided.

JUDGES 4:5

Deborah held court—it may not seem like a terribly significant statement, but it is. It means the people of Israel came to Deborah as their judge. They trusted her wisdom to sort through tough matters. They trusted her discernment to determine what was right. Deborah was treated with respect equal to that of the male judges.

Deborah is one of many historical women who prove that as long as women have been around, they've been capable of leading. One of England's greatest monarchs was Elizabeth I. Or consider her African contemporaries, Amina of Nigeria and Mbande Nzinga of Angola. Or how about military leaders, like Joan of Arc, or leaders of contemporary movements, like Malala Yousafzai, who is the youngest Nobel Prize laureate and advocate for girls' education. Or Hatshepsut, who peacefully ruled Egypt hundreds of years before Deborah lived! We have a lot of fine examples of female leadership, ladies.

What qualities do good leaders possess?

Day 43

In the days when the judges ruled, there was a famine in the land. So a man from Bethlehem in Judah, together with his wife and two sons, went to live for a while in the country of Moab. The man's name was Elimelek, his wife's name was Naomi, and the names of his two sons were Mahlon and Kilion.

RUTH 1:1–2A

We've been getting some of the political highlights of this era in Israel's history—stories of the great rulers and deliverers who lived in the time after Israel entered the promised land. But our next women aren't military, political, or religious leaders. This is just the story of a family. Although, spoiler alert, this family will become politically powerful later on.

Only two books of the sixty-six in the Bible are named after women, and Naomi, Orpah, and Ruth star in one of them. First, we meet Naomi, the matriarch. These verses appear pretty simple on the surface, but they are oddly silent about the underlying feelings of dislike and suspicion that existed between the Israelites and the Moabites. That key information is important to unlock the full message of the book of Ruth.

Ruth and Naomi's story hints at God's great love for *all* people. He had chosen Israel, but his coming gospel was for everyone, and Ruth shows us that this was God's plan all along. Be encouraged, beloved, that God's heart beats for *you*, no matter who you are or where you come from.

What evidence have you seen that proves that God cares for all people?

Day 44

After they had lived there about
ten years, both Mahlon and Kilion
also died, and Naomi was left without
her two sons and her husband.
RUTH 1:4B–5

That's a very sad verse right there. Naomi was left without her sons and her husband. For many millennia of history and throughout many cultures, a woman had very little means to support herself without male relatives. Childlessness was seen as a curse. Naomi suddenly went from a married mother of two to a childless widow. As we see from her words later, she felt empty.

While our situation may never look exactly like Naomi's, there will be times when we feel emptied out and stripped down. There will be times when we feel broken. To combat feelings of despair, we can remind ourselves of important truths. God loves you. God has a plan for your life, and it isn't for you to remain broken.

The pain is real, and it's okay to acknowledge it. Ignoring it doesn't help you move on. But we can continue to battle our brokenness with truth, and in so doing, reclaim our joy.

During hard times it's especially important to remind yourselves of important truths about God. What truths to you need to be reminded of today?

To combat feelings of despair, we can remind ourselves of important truths. God loves you. God has a plan for your life, and it isn't for you to remain broken.

Day 45

When Naomi heard in Moab that the Lord had come to the aid of his people by providing food for them, she and her daughters-in-law prepared to return home from there. With her two daughters-in-law she left the place where she had been living and set out on the road that would take them back to the land of Judah.

RUTH 1:6–7

Naomi had left Israel because there'd been a bad famine in the land, and now, after many years in Moab, it was time to return home.

Going home can mean many different things. It can be returning to your physical home after an absence. It can mean reuniting with your family, wherever they may be. It can mean returning to a place where you have bonds, like the church you grew up in or the school you love. Going home can also mean returning to our roots in our relationships with God.

For every person who calls Jesus her Savior, there was a time when we were deeply in love with him and when we deeply

understood God's love for us. It's easy to get caught up in the busyness of life—even the busyness of church life—and wander away from this "home base" with God. The good news is that we can return whenever we want! We can always pray for God to reignite our sense of home with him, and he will.

Describe what the comforts of home feel like to you. What type of things give you a feeling of stability?

Day 46

But Ruth replied, "Don't urge me to leave you or to turn back from you. Where you go I will go, and where you stay I will stay. Your people will be my people and your God my God. Where you die I will die, and there I will be buried. May the LORD deal with me, be it ever so severely, if even death separates you and me." When Naomi realized that Ruth was determined to go with her, she stopped urging her.

RUTH 1:16–18

This, perhaps more than any other passage, reveals Ruth's heart. When we contrast her with Orpah, we see how deeply committed Ruth was to Naomi and Naomi's God. She was so committed, she was willing to give up her home and her own people. Ruth knew she had found something better than her birth.

Some people may seem like they have been blessed with absolutely everything. The perfect churchgoing family, parents who completely "get" them, a comfortable financial situation . . . But the truth is, no matter how outwardly perfect anyone's life looks (and we better remind ourselves that everyone has troubles

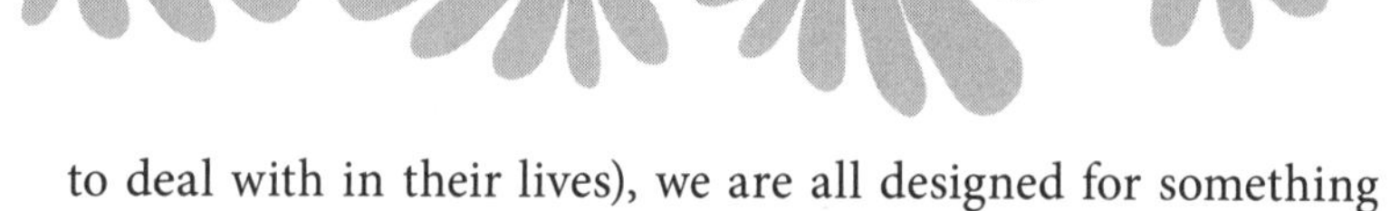

to deal with in their lives), we are all designed for something "better than our birth."

And that's because the world we're all born into is marred by sin. Our world is warped because sin has entered it. It's not as God originally designed it. So, deep down in all our hearts, we're longing for that sinless world, which will return when Jesus does. How cool is that? We were designed for something greater!

Glance back and read the Bible passage. How would you describe Ruth's heart toward Naomi?

Day 47

Now Naomi had a relative on her husband's side, a man of standing from the clan of Elimelek, whose name was Boaz. And Ruth the Moabite said to Naomi, "Let me go to the fields and pick up the leftover grain behind anyone in whose eyes I find favor." Naomi said to her, "Go ahead, my daughter."

RUTH 2:1–2

There were provisions written into the law for the poor in Israel. They were to be allowed to "glean" in the fields behind the field hands while they harvested, which is exactly what Ruth is asking to do.

Ruth is an excellent role model for us in so many ways. We might think that all our awesome biblical women are very powerful (like Deborah), from well-connected families (like Miriam), or that they possessed material wealth (like Sarah). But none of these things is true of Ruth. Yet she is perfectly willing to do whatever honorable activity she must in order to support herself and her mother-in-law. In Ruth, we see that humble means can be noble means.

Caring for those we love and having servants' hearts is never beneath us. Getting our hands dirty (proverbially or literally) through hard work isn't beneath us. Willingness to do these things shows humility that honors God.

Ruth showed that she was willing to work hard to provide for herself and Naomi. Why is being a hard worker important no matter what you are doing?

Day 48

Boaz asked the overseer of his harvesters, "Who does that young woman belong to?" The overseer replied, "She is the Moabite who came back from Moab with Naomi."

RUTH 2:5–6

Now we meet the leading man of Ruth's story, Boaz. He's a great biblical man to study, but we'll get to that later. First, can we take a moment to notice this cool "God moment"? Among all his workers in all his fields, Boaz happens to notice Ruth. And he takes enough notice that he decides to ask about her. If he hadn't noticed her or shown interest in who she was, this entire story might have looked quite different. And Israel's history might have even been different.

Perhaps most of our days are filled with our regular day- to-day activities. But, like Ruth and Boaz have here, some of our days will have God-orchestrated intersections that change our lives. Can you look back on your life up to this point and name a couple of those? Those times when something "happened" to fall into place in just such a way that it helped shape your life from that point forward? These moments don't occur by accident.

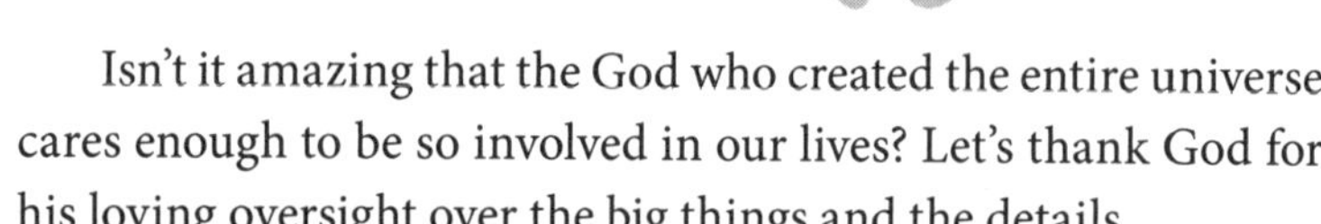

Isn't it amazing that the God who created the entire universe cares enough to be so involved in our lives? Let's thank God for his loving oversight over the big things and the details.

Can you recall a time when it was obvious that God was involved in the details of your life? What happened?

Day 49

Watch the field where the men are harvesting, and follow along after the women. I have told the men not to lay a hand on you. And whenever you are thirsty, go and get a drink from the water jars the men have filled.
RUTH 2:9

Boaz made it a priority to protect Ruth. He told his male workers not to touch Ruth. The fact that he felt this necessary highlights once again Ruth's vulnerability in her current situation. Perhaps some men would try to take advantage of the fact that Ruth didn't have a husband, father, or brother to defend her. So Boaz steps in and puts the men on notice that *he* will step in if Ruth is harmed. He's showing her an immense amount of care—and she's practically a stranger!

Even though we enjoy much more social freedom than the women of Ruth's day, we can still be very vulnerable in some ways. Every young woman should learn some self-defense basics, at least, to help her be more empowered and less physically vulnerable. But what about the quality of protectiveness in a partner?

When protectiveness comes from a place of control, it can be a negative. But when it's coming from a place of love and respect—like the kind of care Boaz showed—it's a very good thing. We should be looking for a partner who cares about our physical, emotional, and spiritual well-being.

Who are the people you feel safe with? Are there people in your life who make you feel unsafe? Who can you talk to if you feel unsafe?

Day 50

Now Boaz, with whose women you have worked, is a relative of ours. Tonight he will be winnowing barley on the threshing floor. Wash, put on perfume, and get dressed in your best clothes. Then go down to the threshing floor, but don't let him know you are there until he has finished eating and drinking. When he lies down, note the place where he is lying. Then go and uncover his feet and lie down. He will tell you what to do.

RUTH 3:2–4

This is an interesting thing Naomi is asking of her daughter-in-law. She tells Ruth to prepare herself as if for marriage and go meet Boaz in private after he's finished with his evening of harvest celebration. I mean . . . can we all agree this isn't the standard advice most mothers would give to their daughters?

But Naomi's instructions highlight something important. Being bold isn't always an immoral thing. Ruth's act was definitely gutsy, but her behavior is not at all called out as wrong. In fact, Ruth is often pointed to as an example of a very godly

biblical woman. She is bold when the situation calls for boldness, gentle when gentleness is best, and is at all times striving to behave honorably. That's quite a role model for us!

If you could, which part of Ruth's character would you inject a little more of into your own life? Do you want to become less timid? Or are you working on upping your gentleness factor when the situation calls for it? Ask God to help you grow in the areas you'd like to most!

Does your personality lean toward boldness or gentleness? Or does it fall in between?

Day 51

So Boaz took Ruth and she became his wife. When he made love to her, the Lord enabled her to conceive, and she gave birth to a son.
RUTH 4:13

So maybe we wouldn't normally have a devotion that dives right into Boaz and Ruth's bedroom. It feels a little personal, after all. But this son Ruth conceives is important to note. His name was Obed, and he was the father of Jesse, and Jesse was the father of King David. Through David's line, the promised Messiah, Jesus, would be born. So not only had Ruth become an Israelite, but God had grafted her, a Moabite, into Jesus's family tree.

Stories like Ruth's are special. Even though it's found in the Old Testament, Ruth's story hints at God's full plan. He had always planned to redeem, not just the Israelite people, but *all* people through Jesus. No matter someone's nationality, skin color, family history, or previous religious association, Jesus's love is for them. It's for you. It's for all of us.

This idea was revolutionary in the time just after Jesus's life on Earth ended and the apostles began to share the gospel with

people who weren't Jewish. And it's pretty revolutionary now. *All people* have the love of Jesus made available to them, and Ruth was a foreshadowing of that fact.

What qualities does Ruth have that you admire?

Day 52

[Elkanah] had two wives; one was called Hannah and the other Peninnah. Peninnah had children, but Hannah had none.

1 SAMUEL 1:2

We're fast-forwarding some and we've come to the very end of the period of Israel's judges, and this short verse gives us a sad, succinct introduction to Hannah. Her husband had two wives, and Hannah was "the one with none." We can guess that a situation like this—one man, two wives—would usually lead to a fair amount of rivalry at the best of times. But when one woman was able to have children and the other wasn't, it had to have been drastically worse.

Dealing with rivalry isn't easy, especially when you're the one with none. Maybe you often feel competition with a sibling, and that sibling excels at something you don't. That's a tough situation. Maybe sometimes we gain a victory and become "the one with some," but those victories are fleeting. If we're chasing those, we'll never be completely satisfied.

The long-term solution is to understand that we aren't created for comparison. You were created with unique gifts to use,

particular trials to overcome, and specific triumphs to celebrate. When you embrace your own path and avoid falling into the comparison trap, you can find contentment, as well as the motivation to be the very best *you* possible.

Why is it best to avoid the comparison trap?

Day 53

In her deep anguish Hannah prayed to the LORD, weeping bitterly. And she made a vow, saying, "LORD Almighty, if you will only look on your servant's misery and remember me, and not forget your servant but give her a son, then I will give him to the LORD for all the days of his life, and no razor will ever be used on his head."

1 SAMUEL 1:10–11

Hannah went to God very openly. She cried. She wept. She may have even wailed. She let him see every bit of her dis- tress. She came to him open-hearted and vulnerable.

Sometimes we get the idea that we need to be proper with God. Perhaps we've learned that showing someone respect means being on our best behavior, so we button our lips, zip up our hearts, and approach God with a detached cool that displays our respect for him.

Hey, it's important to respect God. Absolutely! But perhaps we need to tweak our idea of what "respect" looks like. Reverence, sure. But also openness. Transparency that says, "I trust you. You see me, you love me, and this is the reality of what I'm experiencing right now. It's ugly, and I trust you to love me through the ugliness." To be so open with someone is to respect them deeply. What if we always approached God with all our hearts? What if we always approached God the way Hannah did?

Is there an area in your life that might prompt you to pray with the fervency that Hannah did? If so, describe the situation.

Day 54

Early the next morning they arose and worshiped before the LORD and then went back to their home at Ramah. Elkanah made love to his wife Hannah, and the LORD remembered her. So in the course of time Hannah became pregnant and gave birth to a son. She named him Samuel, saying, "Because I asked the LORD for him."

1 SAMUEL 1:19–20

Okay, so we're back in a biblical bedroom. Sorry about that. But since Hannah's whole story centers around her infertility, it's kind of hard to avoid. And this is a happy turn of events, after all. Hannah is finally getting what she so desperately wanted. She gets a baby!

Look, it's important to manage our expectations. It's important to make sure we understand the hard truth that we don't always get what we want. Sometimes God says no. There is no magic formula to ensure God always says yes, and even if there were, we'd probably want to be very wary of such a thing.

But, even after we've triggered all the gloomy truth bombs

we can possibly detonate, there's another truth to consider. Sometimes God makes miracles happen. Sometimes God *says yes* and makes the impossible possible. While we don't want to expect that of God every time we ask for something, it's true that sometimes, that's what God does.

Have you ever been pleasantly surprised by a happy turn of events? What happened that surprised you?

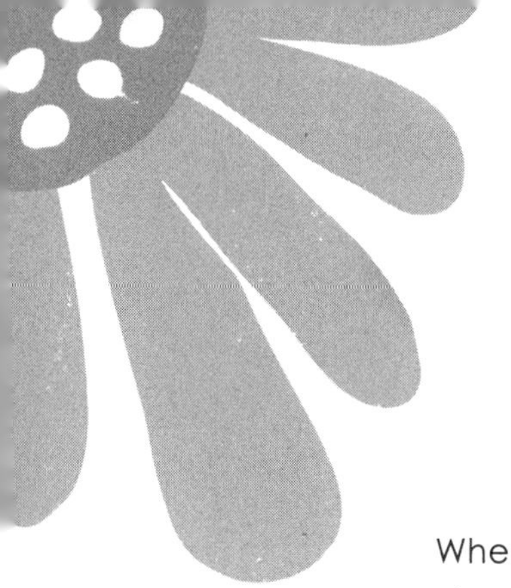

Day 55

When Mordecai learned of all that had been done, he tore his clothes, put on sackcloth and ashes, and went out into the city, wailing loudly and bitterly. But he went only as far as the king's gate, because no one clothed in sackcloth was allowed to enter it. In every province to which the edict and order of the king came, there was great mourning among the Jews, with fasting, weeping and wailing. Many lay in sackcloth and ashes.

ESTHER 4:1–3

We've skipped ahead in time, and now the kingdom of Judah is under the rule of the Persians. If you haven't read Esther, do it! It's ten short chapters, and it's quite the roller coaster. Here, Mordecai was mourning because one of Xerxes's close advisors had hatched a plot to destroy the Jews because of a personal grudge against Mordecai.

This isn't the first and it wouldn't be the last time God's people would have a target on their backs. Even now, Jesus's church often experiences a double standard of judgment and ridicule in the most accepting cultures and horrible persecution and martyrdom in those cultures and political climates where Christianity is not tolerated. The world will always seek to destroy God's followers.

But it's important that we don't become victims. Jesus warned us to expect persecution and opposition (John 15:20–27). Part of following him is accepting this burden with grace—even when it feels impossible!

How do you think God wants you to deal with opposition?

Day 56

Mordecai told [Hathak] everything that had happened to him, including the exact amount of money Haman had promised to pay into the royal treasury for the destruction of the Jews. He also gave him a copy of the text of the edict for their annihilation . . . to show to Esther and explain it to her, and he told him to instruct her to go into the king's presence to beg for mercy and plead with him for her people.

ESTHER 4:7–8

The danger to Esther and Mordecai's people was real. Mordecai made sure Esther understood that the Jewish people faced genocide. Not only that, if Esther did what Mordecai asked, her life would be directly threatened. Most of us probably can't begin to understand the terror they must have felt.

And yet, people living in the world today face similar fears. Some people are in danger because their race or culture is in the crosshairs of a different people group. Some people face the threat of violence because of their religious beliefs, and that includes the many Christians around the world who face the possibility of death just for confessing the name of Jesus.

It's easy to forget about these realities today. But it's important to make ourselves remember those who face terror and danger every day. We can pray for their safety and their hearts. This helps us appreciate our own situations and keep our trials in perspective!

Why is it important to pray for our brothers and sisters in Christ who are facing persecution for their faith?

Day 57

When Esther's words were reported to Mordecai, he sent back this answer: "Do not think that because you are in the king's house you alone of all the Jews will escape. For if you remain silent at this time, relief and deliverance for the Jews will arise from another place, but you and your father's family will perish. And who knows but that you have come to your royal position for such a time as this?"

ESTHER 4:12–14

These are powerful words from Mordecai, and perhaps the most famous from Esther's story: *for such a time as this*. Mordecai's challenge might be the most famous part of his speech, but did you notice his faithful confession just before his challenge? He feels sure the Jews will be delivered. Why? Because he trusts God will always save a remnant of his people, no matter what they face. But Mordecai was wise enough to recognize that it probably wasn't a coincidence Esther had become queen.

Mordecai's basic point of view still applies to us today. God's purposes will be accomplished no matter what because he's God.

But are we willing to say, “Yes, I’m here” and be part of that plan? That was Mordecai’s challenge to Esther, and that’s a question we can ask ourselves daily.

Are you willing to be used by God to advance his purposes? What might that look like at your church, school, and extracurricular activities?

God's purposes will
be accomplished
no matter what
because he's God.

Day 58

On the third day Esther put on her royal robes and stood in the inner court of the palace, in front of the king's hall. The king was sitting on his royal throne in the hall, facing the entrance. When he saw Queen Esther standing in the court, he was pleased with her and held out to her the gold scepter that was in his hand. So Esther approached and touched the tip of the scepter.

ESTHER 5:1–2

Have you noticed something unusual about the verses from Esther? There are literally no mentions of God. It's true. Esther is the only book of the Bible that doesn't explicitly mention God. And yet, God is obviously in the story. Esther's big risk was in approaching the king without being summoned. He was within his legal rights to execute her for it. But when she did, he was "coincidentally" in a favorable mood, and he extended mercy to her. In any other book of the Bible, this verse might say, "But God softened Xerxes's heart toward Esther." Here, we don't get that commentary.

And maybe that's why Esther is such a relatable book. God is there, shifting all the pieces into place. But he's also invisible. And that's how God is for us a lot of the time. We know he's there, but we don't often get insight into exactly what he's doing or thinking. Esther's story encourages us that, even though we can't know God's behind-the-scene thoughts all the time, we *can* see him moving clearly, even when he's not mentioned by name.

It took bravery for Esther to approach the king without being summoned. In what areas of your life do you feel God prompting you to be brave?

Day 59

King Xerxes replied to Queen Esther and to Mordecai the Jew, "Because Haman attacked the Jews, I have given his estate to Esther, and they have impaled him on the pole he set up. Now write another decree in the king's name in behalf of the Jews as seems best to you, and seal it with the king's signet ring—for no document written in the king's name and sealed with his ring can be revoked."

ESTHER 8:7–8

Things worked out very well for Esther, Mordecai, and all the Jewish people. Esther was able to save her people, and the advisor who had it out for Mordecai was punished—harshly. It was the best possible outcome for a vulnerable people who had been facing extinction.

It's true that God's people will often have a target on their backs because the world wants to destroy what God wants to build up. But we must also remember that God is the great deliverer. He doesn't ignore us when we cry for help. Even if the earthly trials we're facing are difficulties we must go through, for

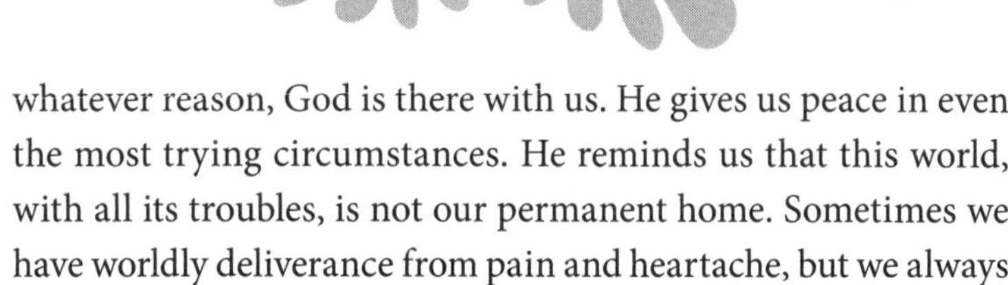

whatever reason, God is there with us. He gives us peace in even the most trying circumstances. He reminds us that this world, with all its troubles, is not our permanent home. Sometimes we have worldly deliverance from pain and heartache, but we always have eternal, spiritual deliverance.

Have you ever felt at peace even when you were going through a hard time? If so, describe what it felt like.

Day 60

In the time of Herod king of Judea there was a priest named Zechariah, who belonged to the priestly division of Abijah; his wife Elizabeth was also a descendant of Aaron. Both of them were righteous in the sight of God, observing all the Lord's commands and decrees blamelessly. But they were childless because Elizabeth was not able to conceive, and they were both very old.

LUKE 1:5–7

We've made it to the New Testament! There are a lot more women in the New Testament than many people realize, and if we're going chronologically, Elizabeth should be the first one we look at.

The beginning of Elizabeth and Zechariah's story is another that falls under the category of "things we might not like to think about." They upheld the Law of Moses as best they could and were faithful followers of God, but they still had not been blessed with a child.

It's not always easy to trust that God knows best in these situations. When we want something badly, that desire can crowd

out everything else in our minds. We have to let the truth—that God is always working all things to our good (Rom. 8:28)—speak louder than our desires. God has a good plan for each of us. We can trust him and his timing!

What does it mean to "trust God's timing"?

Day 61

[The angel said] "Your wife Elizabeth will bear you a son, and you are to call him John. He will be a joy and delight to you, and many will rejoice because of his birth, for he will be great in the sight of the Lord... He will bring back many of the people of Israel to the Lord their God."

LUKE 1:13B–15A, 16

Elizabeth's story didn't end with an unfulfilled desire. Just like the angel proclaimed, Elizabeth became the mother of John the Baptist, who was an important trailblazer ahead of Jesus's earthly ministry. We have so many miraculous conceptions recorded in the Bible, we might think of them as much more common than they were. But make no mistake—this event was far outside of the "norm." In this case, God's plan was much bigger than the norm.

Sometimes God's plan for our lives turns the norm on its head too. Think about your plans for your future. How many of those plans are based on doing what's expected of you? Sometimes those expectations are great. Other times, we haven't really put in the thought or prayer to discern if we're just

plodding in a certain direction because it's our norm or if that's really where God wants us. Take some time to pray about it now, and see what you discover!

What areas in your life do you need God's guidance and direction? Write those in your prayer journal and make praying about them a priority.

Day 62

After this his wife Elizabeth became pregnant and for five months remained in seclusion. "The Lord has done this for me," she said. "In these days he has shown his favor and taken away my disgrace among the people."
LUKE 1:24–25

Can you imagine what it was like to be in Elizabeth's shoes? She went from an elderly, barren woman who considered herself "disgraced" among the people to the mother of a miracle child. Just like that, her entire identity had changed.

God is in the habit of doing that. Our relationship with Jesus brings us from darkness to light. We were blind, now we see. We were dead in our sins, now we live. Believing in Jesus changes our identity in these ways and others.

That's a pretty deep thought! But the apostle Paul wrote about it a lot—becoming a new man (or woman) in Christ. When you're struggling with something—anything from a bad attitude to a serious situation—you can find hope, strength, and encouragement in this fact. You are a new creature in Jesus, with a totally new identity as God's beloved daughter.

How does Elizabeth's story encourage you?

Our relationship with
Jesus brings us from
darkness to light.

Day 63

In the sixth month of Elizabeth's pregnancy, God sent the angel Gabriel to Nazareth, a town in Galilee, to a virgin pledged to be married to a man named Joseph, a descendant of David. The virgin's name was Mary. The angel went to her and said, "Greetings, you who are highly favored! The Lord is with you."

LUKE 1:26–28

We've reached the most famous woman in the Bible—actually, one of the most famous women in all history! Mary, the mother of Jesus. For two thousand years, people have been reading about, writing about, and painting portraits of Mary. By all accounts, she was a young woman. She wasn't a princess or a prophet or a military leader. She was just a normal girl.

Isn't it cool to think about how much God entrusted to this regular girl? He judged her capable of shouldering this sizable burden—and honor. She wasn't disqualified because she was young or because she was normal. God looked at her heart and said, "Yes. You're the one."

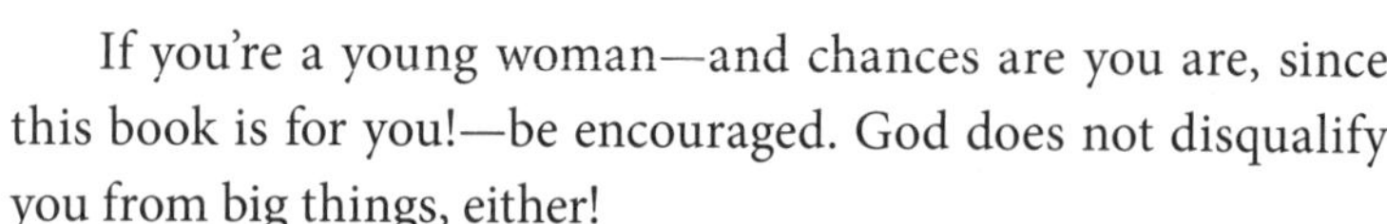

If you're a young woman—and chances are you are, since this book is for you!—be encouraged. God does not disqualify you from big things, either!

Glance back at today's Bible verses. What two things did Gabriel say when he greeted Mary? What could you accomplish if you were convinced that you are favored and God is with you?

Day 64

Mary was greatly troubled at his words and wondered what kind of greeting this might be. But the angel said to her, "Do not be afraid, Mary; you have found favor with God. You will conceive and give birth to a son, and you are to call him Jesus. He will be great and will be called the Son of the Most High. The Lord God will give him the throne of his father David, and he will reign over Jacob's descendants forever; his kingdom will never end."

LUKE 1:29–33

If most people had sat down to write the plan for mankind's redemption, it probably wouldn't have looked much like what God's plan was. We tend to like superheroes—people who are big, strong, and wear capes and masks. Our culture glorifies those who are talented and beautiful, wealthy and powerful.

But God chose a young woman to give birth to a baby boy, and that boy carried the weight of mankind's redemption on his very human shoulders. Also? Though the boy was human, he was also God himself. So the great big God of the universe took on human frailty in order to make this plan work.

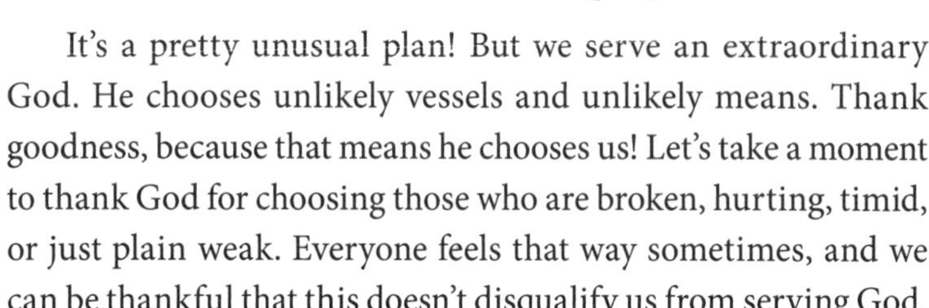

It's a pretty unusual plan! But we serve an extraordinary God. He chooses unlikely vessels and unlikely means. Thank goodness, because that means he chooses us! Let's take a moment to thank God for choosing those who are broken, hurting, timid, or just plain weak. Everyone feels that way sometimes, and we can be thankful that this doesn't disqualify us from serving God.

Why do you think God often chooses ordinary people to accomplish his work?

Day 65

[The angel said] "Even Elizabeth your relative is going to have a child in her old age, and she who was said to be unable to conceive is in her sixth month. For no word from God will ever fail." "I am the Lord's servant," Mary answered. "May your word to me be fulfilled." Then the angel left her.

LUKE 1:36–38

We've seen a lot of miraculous conceptions in the Bible so far and several declarations from angels beforehand, letting the parent-to-be know it was about to happen. What we don't see as often is a response like Mary's. She responded in faith, not doubt. She said, essentially, "I belong to God—let your words come true." That's a profound demonstration of faith, especially when you consider that Mary was unmarried. The angel's prophecy was even more unbelievable than most. Not only was she to conceive a child, she was to do so while remaining a virgin. What?

Maybe that is what God saw in this regular young woman—the kind of faith that believes in the impossible and the kind of trust that says, "I'm yours, God. Use me as you will." If you're like most people, you could probably use a little more of that kind of faith and trust. Is there an area in your life where you've felt particularly doubtful about trusting God? Spend some time today focused on practicing Mary-like faith in that tough area. God honors those efforts.

What characteristic does Mary have that you'd like to possess?

Day 66

When Elizabeth heard Mary's greeting, the baby leaped in her womb, and Elizabeth was filled with the Holy Spirit. In a loud voice she exclaimed: "Blessed are you among women, and blessed is the child you will bear! But why am I so favored, that the mother of my Lord should come to me? As soon as the sound of your greeting reached my ears, the baby in my womb leaped for joy. Blessed is she who has believed that the Lord would fulfill his promises to her!"

LUKE 1:41–45

This is such a cool moment. Elizabeth and Mary were related, and after Mary had spoken to the angel, she went to see her relative. This was what happened when they met each other. John the Baptist, in utero, leapt at Mary's presence. Crazy!

There was a lot of direct Holy Spirit intervention happening in this moment. And it's no wonder. It was a pretty special moment, never to be repeated again. The Holy Spirit was talking to tiny John and to Elizabeth. While this definitely isn't the norm, have you thought about the fact that you have the same Holy Spirit living inside of you? The Holy Spirit who is God and knows everything.

We take that for granted sometimes. But it's such an awesome truth! When we're feeling alone, discouraged, weak-willed, or unable, we can remember the power of the one who lives in us. He is there to enable, equip, and encourage us. That's amazing!

How can you draw on God's Spirit within you for strength?

Day 67

And Mary said: "My soul glorifies the Lord and my spirit rejoices in God my Savior, for he has been mindful of the humble state of his servant. From now on all generations will call me blessed, for the Mighty One has done great things for me—holy is his name."

LUKE 1:46–49

This is the beginning of a really lovely song from Mary where she expresses everything that is on her heart just after the amazing moment with her relative Elizabeth. It's reminiscent of one of David's psalms.

The written word is an amazing gift. We write to communicate with others, of course, but we also write to pour ourselves out onto the paper—to express what's deep inside and might be difficult to express verbally. Some people do this better in song. Or art. Or dance. Anything that takes what's in our hearts and allows it to be poured outward is accomplishing the same purpose.

How do you best express those deep emotions? Even if you don't feel particularly gifted in any of these areas, journaling is for everyone! When you're writing in a journal, you can feel free to express yourself without ever worrying about showing it to anyone or having anyone else judge it. You can even use the journaling lines in this book to jot down some of your inmost thoughts as you read.

What is your favorite way to express your love for God?

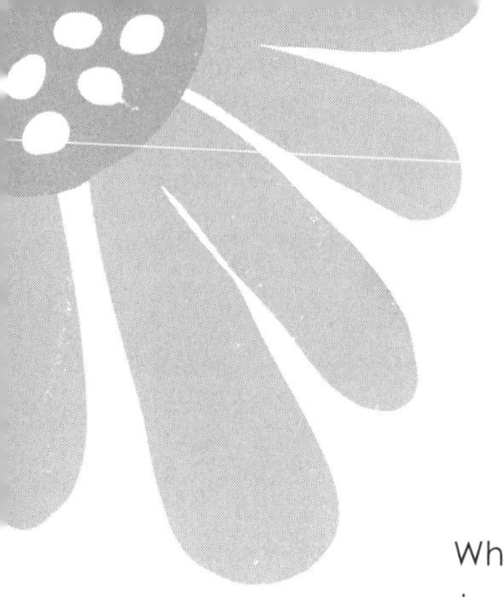

Day 68

When it was time for Elizabeth to have her baby, she gave birth to a son. Her neighbors and relatives heard that the Lord had shown her great mercy, and they shared her joy.
LUKE 1:57–58

That's a simple little statement, but such a powerful one: Elizabeth's neighbors shared her joy. Elizabeth had long wished for a child. She gave birth to a healthy son, and her neighbors rejoiced with her.

Romans 12:15 says: "Rejoice with those who rejoice; mourn with those who mourn." Also a simple statement, but not always easy to practice. Sometimes we poke at those who mourn by blaming them for their hard circumstances or offering cold "comfort" that has the undertones of judgment. And sometimes it's easier to feel jealousy than joy when something amazing or wonderful happens to someone else.

But when we can offer genuine joy for those who rejoice and genuine sorrow for those who mourn, it has a positive effect on our hearts. We grow in empathy, understanding, and selflessness, which makes us more compassionate, loving people. It's an awesome way to reflect Jesus to others!

Can you think of a time when friends or family celebrated with you? How did it feel?

Day 69

On the eighth day they came to circumcise the child, and they were going to name him after his father Zechariah, but his mother spoke up and said, "No! He is to be called John." They said to her, "There is no one among your relatives who has that name." Then they made signs to his father, to find out what he would like to name the child. He asked for a writing tablet, and to everyone's astonishment he wrote, "His name is John."

LUKE 1:59–63

We've shared some thoughts about defying tradition or turning the norm on its head. Elizabeth does it again here by giving her baby son a name not shared by anyone in her or her husband's families.

But you'll notice she didn't "rebel" for the sake of it. She didn't defy expectations because she was desperate to stand out or because she wanted to disrespect her culture. She did it because she was being obedient to God's instructions, delivered through the angel.

It's okay to defy expectations and go against the grain. In fact, sometimes that's exactly what we *must* do. But it's important we do it for the right reasons. Expectations and norms should take a back seat to God's leading, just like they did for Elizabeth and Zechariah.

Do you think Elizabeth was bold or brave to name her son John? If so, why do you feel that way?

Day 70

This is how the birth of Jesus the Messiah came about: His mother Mary was pledged to be married to Joseph, but before they came together, she was found to be pregnant through the Holy Spirit. Because Joseph her husband was faithful to the law, and yet did not want to expose her to public disgrace, he had in mind to divorce her quietly.

MATTHEW 1:18–19

There's a lot to digest here. Joseph and Mary were engaged, which was as good as married in those days. When Mary became pregnant before she and Joseph had gotten married, of course his obvious assumption would be that she had gotten pregnant by another man. In other words, Mary looked a lot like an adulteress. And he was not okay with adultery. But even before he knew the totally unique circumstances of Mary's pregnancy (and that she was, indeed, not an adulteress), he wanted to protect her. He could have made her disgrace public and had her punished as the law prescribed. Instead, he was going to walk away from the engagement ("divorce," as the verse says) quietly. Wow.

Joseph was a good man. He was upright and godly, but he still remained compassionate. While we may be focusing on biblical role models who are women in this book, Joseph is an excellent role model for us too. It can be really difficult to maintain the balance of righteousness and compassion, but Joseph gives us a great example of how to do just that.

Joseph displayed several excellent qualities. Which one most inspires you?

Day 71

So [the shepherds] hurried off and found Mary and Joseph, and the baby, who was lying in the manger. When they had seen him, they spread the word concerning what had been told them about this child, and all who heard it were amazed at what the shepherds said to them. But Mary treasured up all these things and pondered them in her heart.

LUKE 2:16–19

Joseph was visited by an angel and got clued in about the very special family he and Mary were about to begin. They did end up marrying, and Joseph was there for the birth of the Messiah. Which brings us to this very familiar stable.

Mary was in the habit of treasuring and pondering things in her heart. Wise girl. Especially when you consider the extraordinary events of her life, it's no wonder Mary had a particular need to really chew on these wild happenings. Her thoughtful temperament probably equipped her to handle her special role with grace.

We're bombarded with new information all the time. We ask our brains—and our hearts—to process *a lot*. And while all of it may be more mundane than the things Mary needed to process in her life, it's no wonder that we get fatigued.

We would be wise to adopt Mary's practice of quiet reflection. It allows our minds to slow down, process, evaluate, compare, and digest.

Journaling, quiet reflection, and setting aside time to review your week are all ways you could get in the habit of taking time to ponder things. Which one is most appealing to you?

Day 72

There was also a prophet, Anna, the daughter of Penuel, of the tribe of Asher. She was very old; she had lived with her husband seven years after her marriage, and then was a widow until she was eighty-four. She never left the temple but worshiped night and day, fasting and praying.

LUKE 2:36–37

Another female prophet! Anna doesn't have a ton of space devoted to her story, but she was a pretty cool lady. She was married for a relatively short time, then her husband died. She lived the rest of her life as a widow and devoted most—maybe all—of her time to worshiping God. Wow!

Anna is a great encouragement for those who feel called to devote their lives to God's service instead of marriage or family. But even those of us who do want to be married and have children can adopt a little bit of Anna's spirit.

There are numerous ways to serve the kingdom of God. Maybe it means helping out at your church, or maybe it means ministering to that friend who has been asking about God lately.

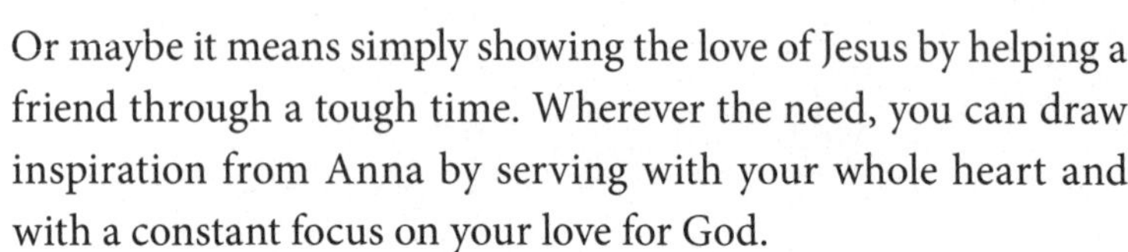

Or maybe it means simply showing the love of Jesus by helping a friend through a tough time. Wherever the need, you can draw inspiration from Anna by serving with your whole heart and with a constant focus on your love for God.

What's one way you can serve the kingdom this week?

Day 73

Coming up to them at that very moment, [Anna] gave thanks to God and spoke about the child to all who were looking forward to the redemption of Jerusalem.

LUKE 2:38

Anna was a legitimate prophet. She knew who this baby boy was the moment his parents brought him into the temple courtyard. And she didn't stay quiet about it. She marched up to Jesus's family, thanked God, and preached about the redemption to come. Not only was she legit, she was bold.

Sometimes we shy away from sharing our faith with others. That may be because a lot of people have had bad experiences with "church people" or because we think we have to preach fire and brimstone and judgment on people. But there's another option. Instead of preaching judgment, we can share our hope, like Anna.

What's the difference? Well, the gospel does require us to turn away from our sins. But the main message of Jesus is that he saved us because he loves us. When we realize what Jesus did for us, turning away from things that displease God comes more naturally—no brimstone required.

Do you have any hesitations when it comes to sharing your faith? What steps can you take to be more comfortable talking about your faith?

Day 74

Near the cross of Jesus stood his mother, his mother's sister, Mary the wife of Clopas, and Mary Magdalene. When Jesus saw his mother there, and the disciple whom he loved standing nearby, he said to her, "Woman, here is your son," and to the disciple, "Here is your mother." From that time on, this disciple took her into his home.

JOHN 19:25–27

We've skipped through the rest of Jesus's ministry for a moment to get one final picture of Mary, Jesus's mother. While Jesus died on the cross, Mary was there. Can you imagine her grief? Even if she fully understood who he was and what would happen next, her heart must have been breaking.

In those final moments of Jesus's life, he thought of his mother. John was Jesus's best friend, and before Jesus died, he made it clear he wanted John to become like a son to Mary and take care of her in her old age. Mary had other sons, but Jesus was asking John to take *his* place. And John fulfilled his duty—from that time on, Mary became a part of John's household. Friends who are like family are a precious gift. Having heart friends like that in no way takes away from your actual family. But if we're lucky enough to have friends who love and support us like family should, we can embrace that blessing. Do you have any friends in your life who are like family? Take a moment to pray for them and to thank God for bringing them into your life.

Even during the final moments of his life, Jesus was thinking about Mary's well-being. What does this teach you about Jesus's character?

Day 75

Now he had to go through Samaria. So he came to a town in Samaria called Sychar, near the plot of ground Jacob had given to his son Joseph. Jacob's well was there, and Jesus, tired as he was from the journey, sat down by the well. It was about noon. When a Samaritan woman came to draw water, Jesus said to her, "Will you give me a drink?"

JOHN 4:4–7

To understand the New Testament stories that mention Samaritans, it's important to get a little history lesson. Let's fill in some blanks.

Samaritans and Jews shared Israelite ancestry, but after Israel split into two kingdoms, they started to go their separate ways. By Jesus's time, there was a lot of tension between these two groups. In short, Samaritans were "other," as far as the Jews were concerned. They were an unclean, "impure" people.

Isn't it crazy that these kinds of tensions have existed for so long? We still deal with them today all over the world. But the love of Jesus is a tremendous force of reconciliation. Jesus reached across the divide to the "others" of his day.

A simple act of kindness like Jesus's reaches across the divide. A smile, a kind word, a show of concern—these small acts demonstrate to people that you don't see them as "other." Though you may be up against some strong cultural tensions, you can show that you care by making the first move.

What are some practical ways you can "reach across the divide" in your school and community?

Day 76

The Samaritan woman said to him, "You are a Jew and I am a Samaritan woman. How can you ask me for a drink?" (For Jews do not associate with Samaritans.) Jesus answered her, "If you knew the gift of God and who it is that asks you for a drink, you would have asked him and he would have given you living water."

JOHN 4:9–10

There was a lot that could have potentially separated Jesus from the woman at the well. The fact that she was a woman, for one—Jesus and this woman were not considered social equals in biblical times. And there's obviously the fact that she was a Samaritan. Jesus could have turned away, ignored the woman, or even been rude to her—that's what his culture would have expected. But even early in his ministry, Jesus is seen breaking through all those barriers to reach out to this woman drawing water.

There is nothing that disqualifies us from receiving God's grace. There is no sin in your past—no boundaries of culture, ethnicity, or gender—that separates you from redemption. It's

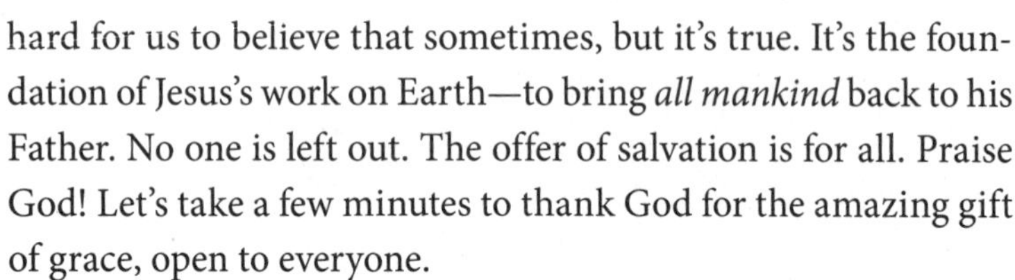

hard for us to believe that sometimes, but it's true. It's the foundation of Jesus's work on Earth—to bring *all mankind* back to his Father. No one is left out. The offer of salvation is for all. Praise God! Let's take a few minutes to thank God for the amazing gift of grace, open to everyone.

Jesus broke with cultural norms to speak with the Samaritan woman. How do you think she felt about her interaction with Jesus?

There is nothing that disqualifies us from receiving God's grace. There is no sin in your past—no boundaries of culture, ethnicity, or gender—that separates you from redemption.

Day 77

"Sir," the woman said, "you have nothing to draw with and the well is deep. Where can you get this living water? Are you greater than our father Jacob, who gave us the well?" . . . Jesus answered, "Everyone who drinks this water will be thirsty again, but whoever drinks the water I give them will never thirst. Indeed, the water I give them will become in them a spring of water welling up to eternal life." The woman said to him, "Sir, give me this water so that I won't get thirsty and have to keep coming here to draw water."

JOHN 4:11–15

To be fair, Jesus was speaking in riddles a little bit. He told stories in such a way that it was easy to miss the full truth of what he was saying if his listeners weren't carefully weighing his words. Most people at this time didn't know he was the Son of God—that his stories were so much more than just interesting tales.

We're in the position of knowing who Jesus is. But even though we understand exactly who he is and we pay careful attention to his words, we *still* miss the spiritual significance of his messages sometimes. Like the woman at the well, we focus on the practical matters and miss the spiritual truth beneath the surface.

Let's be careful not to get swept up in the practical so much that we miss the spiritual. Let's make sure we're listening carefully to Jesus's spiritual truths, even as the busyness of practical matters tries to grab our attention.

What are practical ways you can pay attention to spiritual truths?

Day 78

He told her, "Go, call your husband and come back." "I have no husband," she replied. Jesus said to her, "You are right when you say you have no husband. The fact is, you have had five husbands, and the man you now have is not your husband. What you have just said is quite true."

JOHN 4:16–18

Ouch. Jesus didn't tiptoe around the truth. He called out the woman at the well quite plainly. She must have felt like she was standing naked before this Jewish stranger as he pointed out her less-than-stellar behavior when it came to men. Jesus was not harsh with the woman, but we can still understand how embarrassed she must have felt.

There's really no hiding our misdeeds from God. Just as Jesus knew all about this woman's situation, he knows all about ours. There's no faking it when your God is omniscient.

Does that freak you out? It's understandable if it does. No one wants their past—or current!—mistakes pointed out. But that's one thing that's so amazing about God. He sees every- thing about us so clearly, even the not-so-great stuff, and *still* he offers us grace, love, and reconciliation. Jesus doesn't want us to continue down a bad path, just like he didn't want the woman to continue down her bad path. That's why we're equipped with the Holy Spirit's help and guidance. We just need to follow his leading!

Why was it necessary for Jesus to lead this woman to the uncomfortable truth about her situation? Why is it so important to address sin in our own life?

Day 79

"Sir," the woman said, "I can see that you are a prophet. Our ancestors worshiped on this mountain, but you Jews claim that the place where we must worship is in Jerusalem."

"Woman," Jesus replied, "believe me, a time is coming when you will worship the Father neither on this mountain nor in Jerusalem . . . Yet a time is coming and has now come when the true worshipers will worship the Father in the Spirit and in truth, for they are the kind of worshipers the Father seeks."

JOHN 4:19–21, 23

Have you ever felt like you have to clean yourself up before approaching Jesus? Have you ever felt like you don't belong in church until you've scrubbed your life of everything God might find displeasing?

If you've ever felt that way, you're not alone. But stories like this one about the Samaritan woman show us that God meets us right where we are. Jesus shared a very deep truth with this woman—even while she was in the midst of some really bad lifestyle choices. Jesus cared about those lifestyle choices, of course, but it didn't stop him from showing compassion to this woman and sharing God's plan with her.

This is important when we feel unworthy. It's also important when we're dealing with others struggling with feelings of unworthiness. Do you know anyone dealing with that right now? You can follow Jesus's example by approaching that person with truth *and* compassion.

Why is it safe to approach Jesus just as you are?

Day 80

The woman said, "I know that Messiah" (called Christ) "is coming. When he comes, he will explain everything to us." Then Jesus declared, "I, the one speaking to you—I am he."

JOHN 4:25–26

This is really amazing. Because we know this truth backward and forward, having read the climax of Jesus's life—his death on the cross and his resurrection—it's easy to skim over this part of the story and not fully grasp its significance.

But look carefully at Jesus's words here. This is his most direct confession of who he is until his trial before Pilate. He is very open with this woman and says plainly to her that he is the Messiah. He hedged with others. He dodged the question sometimes. He didn't even speak this plainly with his own disciples most of the time. But he was open with this Samaritan woman who was living a sinful life. Wow!

She was clearly a seeker of truth. Jesus must have sensed her readiness to hear and digest who he was. Maybe you have a friend who is a "seeker." Have you thought about how you can reach out

to that friend? Take a few moments to pray for an organic opportunity to talk about God with your friend. God often uses us to share deep spiritual truths of who Jesus is!

What evidence do you see that the Samaritan woman was a seeker of the truth?

Day 81

A woman in that town who lived a sinful life learned that Jesus was eating at the Pharisee's house, so she came there with an alabaster jar of perfume. As she stood behind him at his feet weeping, she began to wet his feet with her tears. Then she wiped them with her hair, kissed them and poured perfume on them.

LUKE 7:37–38

Heartbrokenness. It's the only word to describe this woman's attitude as she approaches Jesus. We might wonder what her background was. How did she hear about Jesus? How did she know to come to him for the wholeness she sought? What had she done in her life that branded her as a sinner in the eyes of those surrounding Jesus?

We don't have the answers to these questions. But we do see something so touching, so beautiful, from our Savior in this moment. This story shows us that our pasts are irrelevant. The love of Jesus finds us wherever we are, even when we've made mistakes.

Maybe you have some dark mistakes in your past. If so, you're not alone. People with dark pasts have been coming to Jesus for millennia. He doesn't turn away those seeking to turn their lives around. Maybe that message is for you today, but it's also definitely for all of us as we work to show compassion to those who are hurting.

Has someone ever shown you compassion after you really messed up? How did that make you feel?

Day 82

When the Pharisee who had invited him saw this, he said to himself, "If this man were a prophet, he would know who is touching him and what kind of woman she is—that she is a sinner." Jesus answered him, "Simon, I have something to tell you." "Tell me, teacher," he said . . . "You did not give me any water for my feet, but she wet my feet with her tears and wiped them with her hair. You did not give me a kiss, but this woman, from the time I entered, has not stopped kissing my feet. You did not put oil on my head, but she has poured perfume on my feet."

LUKE 7:39–40, 44B–46

This is an interesting contrast. Jesus is dining in the house of a Pharisee, one of the group that would have been considered the most holy, most righteous of his day. And yet he's being attended to by a woman who is identified only as having a sinful lifestyle.

Jesus knew all about the woman's background, of course. But he didn't want to focus on that. Instead, he highlighted to the

Pharisee what the woman's actions were *now*, not what her past was like.

Our actions matter. We're not saved by our good behavior, but our actions reveal our faith. When we believe that God is real and when we have faith in his Word, we want to behave accordingly. We want to represent him well and truthfully. This woman with a sinful past was taking her first step toward that, and Jesus received it wholeheartedly.

When the Pharisee criticized the woman, how did Jesus respond?

Day 83

"Therefore, I tell you, her many sins have been forgiven—as her great love has shown. But whoever has been forgiven little loves little." Then Jesus said to her, "Your sins are forgiven." The other guests began to say among themselves, "Who is this who even forgives sins?" Jesus said to the woman, "Your faith has saved you; go in peace."

LUKE 7:47–50

Sometimes it's difficult for those who have been through a lot in their lives to feel at home in church. Church can feel like a "perfect" place—one that's holy and sacred. Those who feel marked, whether by their own past sins or by abuse of some kind, sometimes feel like they don't belong.

It's important that we hear the heart of Jesus on this. Jesus did not accept the idea of this woman's sins continuing to stick to her after she'd stepped out in faith. He said she was forgiven. He said she was saved.

We need to bring that heart to church with us. We must remember it for ourselves, surely, and also for anyone else seeking

sanctuary in the arms of God. This was the heart of Jesus two thousand years ago, and it's the heart of Jesus now!

Why do you think those who have been forgiven for many things love deeply?

Day 84

And a woman was there who had been subject to bleeding for twelve years. She had suffered a great deal under the care of many doctors and had spent all she had, yet instead of getting better she grew worse.

MARK 5:25–26

Can you imagine what it must have been like to deal with a chronic illness before the days of modern medicine? Even now, it's no picnic. Literally millions of people deal with these issues on a daily basis. Chronic pain, illness, dysfunctions of the body, special needs, impairments . . . these are all realities for many people. Jesus showed compassion for the sick and the disabled.

Do you know someone who suffers from a chronic illness? Chances are, you do. Maybe *you're* the one dealing with this special type of challenge. Know that Jesus sees you and understands your suffering. If you don't deal with a chronic illness, praise God! A healthy body is a tremendous blessing. But remember in prayer those who do deal with chronic conditions. It can be a heavy burden to bear and very wearying for those who live with it daily—and often for their family members or caretakers.

How can you be of help to those around you who are struggling with an illness?

Day 85

When she heard about Jesus, she came up behind him in the crowd and touched his cloak, because she thought, "If I just touch his clothes, I will be healed."

MARK 5:27–28

This is really deep, when you think about it. This woman had been sick for twelve years. She had been to the top doctors in the land. She had tried absolutely everything she could think of to heal her sickness, to no avail. And yet she had heard about Jesus and she had this secret thought—*if I could only touch his clothes, I'll be healed*. Doctors had been completely unsuccessful, but she believed that the mere touch of Jesus would be enough to heal her. Wow.

This may make us long for the days when Jesus was walking around in his human body on Earth. But his presence is still available to us in a spiritual way through the Holy Spirit. And that presence is powerful, just like it was in Jesus's day when this woman believed (correctly!) that merely touching Jesus would heal her body. Being "in God's presence" means we have an increased awareness of him and his power. It means we

experience him in a way that's bold and true and authentic. It shocks us into a state of worship—an attitude of praise. That's deep too!

After years of discouraging news, why do you think the woman still had faith that Jesus could heal her?

Day 86

Immediately her bleeding stopped and she felt in her body that she was freed from her suffering . . . Then the woman, knowing what had happened to her, came and fell at [Jesus's] feet and, trembling with fear, told him the whole truth. He said to her, "Daughter, your faith has healed you. Go in peace and be freed from your suffering."

MARK 5:29, 33–34

Ah, this is beautiful. Our sick woman's faith that Jesus's touch would heal translated into actual healing for her. After all those years of suffering, her body was whole! Hallelujah!

But we have to be really careful with this. We must both affirm that God absolutely can and does heal (because he still does perform miracles like this!), but we must also acknowledge that even those with faith as deep and true as this sick woman's can suffer illness. Sometimes for their whole lives. Sometimes they even die. We have to be careful that we do not equate this suffering with a lack of faith. Paul mentioned his "thorn in the flesh" that God would not take away in 2 Corinthians 12:7. Job suffered many physical trials, even though it had nothing to do with his faith or lack thereof. Sometimes God allows suffering, and we don't always get to know why.

Have you ever suffered with something—whether physically, spiritually, or emotionally—that God chose not to take away or heal instantaneously? Did you find your faith strengthened through that trial? Take a few moments to express your feelings about it in prayer—even if they're not all pleasant!

In your experience, do you draw closer to God during hard times, or do you struggle to stay close to God when you're suffering? What have you learned from times of struggle?

Day 87

The teachers of the law and the Pharisees brought in a woman caught in adultery. They made her stand before the group and said to Jesus, "Teacher, this woman was caught in the act of adultery. In the Law Moses commanded us to stone such women. Now what do you say?" They were using this question as a trap, in order to have a basis for accusing him.

JOHN 8:3–6

Jesus went against the grain of his culture to reach out to women. Compared to the religious leaders of the day, Jesus was downright revolutionary. These Pharisees sought to publicly shame and punish this woman. If their motivation had been to address a spiritual problem in her life, *maybe* we could understand them a little better. But the verse is clear: They dragged this woman out into public solely to trap Jesus. They wanted to attack their enemy, Jesus, and this woman was acceptable collateral damage.

Even when a person has done something wrong, it's important that we treat her with dignity. Finger-pointing and public

shaming might make us feel superior, but it has little chance of restoring the person in question to right relation- ship with God. Instead, let's be like Jesus. Let's treat people with kindness and respect *first* and then follow with important truths, spoken in love.

Why do you think Jesus often went against the norms of the culture to reach out to women?

Day 88

But Jesus bent down and started to write on the ground with his finger. When they kept on questioning him, he straightened up and said to them, "Let any one of you who is without sin be the first to throw a stone at her." Again he stooped down and wrote on the ground. At this, those who heard began to go away one at a time, the older ones first, until only Jesus was left, with the woman still standing there.

JOHN 8:6–9

This is such a beautiful picture of the heart of Jesus. He knew what was in the minds of the Pharisees. He knew they were seeking to trap him and not at all concerned about this woman or her relationship with God. His heart was to redeem this woman—to save her and not condemn her. Amazing, wild, wonderful grace.

Maybe you have a hard time receiving that grace for yourself. Maybe you feel dark and twisty and irredeemable inside, and you can't imagine Jesus standing in the gap for you, protecting you from your accusers. Or maybe you have a hard time showing this kind of grace to others. Maybe it seems like the world is decaying around you and you're the only one who is getting it right.

If either of those is the case for you right now, you're not alone! Let's take a few moments to pray that our hearts would realign with Jesus's. Let's take a moment to fully grab onto the idea that Jesus's grace is for us and for all those around us, even if they're struggling.

Do you think the Pharisees cared about the well-being of this woman? What evidence do you see that Jesus cared deeply for her?

Day 89

Jesus straightened up and asked her, "Woman, where are they? Has no one condemned you?" "No one, sir," she said. "Then neither do I condemn you," Jesus declared. "Go now and leave your life of sin."

JOHN 8:10–11

People quote Jesus's words in the preceding verses a lot. "Let anyone who is without sin cast the first stone." Those are powerful, wonderful words. But what many people neglect is this next part. Jesus did not condemn the woman, and he did not stone her to death as the law prescribed. But he *did* tell her to leave her life of sin. There's a difference between offering grace and accepting sin.

This is an excruciatingly difficult balance for us to strike. Some of us just want peace, harmony, no confrontation, and no hurt feelings, so we're more likely to be accepting of others' sins. We don't want to rock the boat. Other people are more given to an uncompromising stance, so we find it easier to call out sin and more difficult to show love and compassion.

But we have to show both kindness *and* correction. One

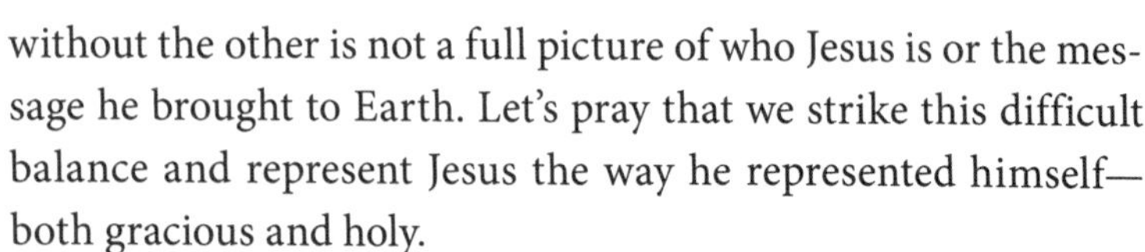

without the other is not a full picture of who Jesus is or the message he brought to Earth. Let's pray that we strike this difficult balance and represent Jesus the way he represented himself—both gracious and holy.

In your own words, describe what it means to be both kind and corrective.

Day 90

As Jesus looked up, he saw the rich putting their gifts into the temple treasury. He also saw a poor widow put in two very small copper coins. "Truly I tell you," he said, "this poor widow has put in more than all the others. All these people gave their gifts out of their wealth; but she out of her poverty put in all she had to live on."

LUKE 21:1–4

Here is another "nameless" woman of the New Testament who is only known by descriptors of her life (poor widow) and what she did (gave two coins). There are many others like her, as Jesus's ministry intersected with the lives of women all the time, and they're all worth reading about.

This widow is a remarkable picture of faith in God's provision. She trusted God to provide for her, so she was willing to give *all* she had. As we see from Jesus's words, the actual monetary value of what she gave was irrelevant. God can use tiny amounts of money—or even no money at all—to do great things. That wasn't the point. The point was that she had so little but she gave *every bit of it.*

That's hard to fathom. Our culture is pretty materialistic. We like our worldly playthings. Can you imagine giving it all over to God if he asked—even the money you had planned to live on? That's crazy, daring, widow-sized faith right there.

What is one way you can be generous toward God and others this week?

Day 91

As Jesus and his disciples
were on their way, he came
to a village where a woman named
Martha opened her home to him.
LUKE 10:38

How cool would it be to be able to say that you were close friends with Jesus during his time on Earth? That's something Martha of Bethany could claim. She shows up in the gospels of Luke and John in a couple different stories.

Martha's name has long been associated with hospitality. We've talked a lot about hospitality and how to bring that spirit with you wherever you go, which is especially important if you're not in a position to entertain in your home. But what are some practical ways to do that?

You can set up a weekly date at a coffee house with a group of friends—to have Bible study, homework time, or just hang-out time. You can plan outings for your friends. They can range from something extravagant like going to an amusement park together, to simple and totally free, like organizing a hike or picnic in the park. You can bring meals (or books or movies!) to

those who are sick. If you do have a home space available for entertaining, you can offer to host birthday parties or other celebrations there.

Who do you know who would benefit from your hospitality right now?

Day 92

She had a sister called Mary, who sat at the Lord's feet listening to what he said.
LUKE 10:39

If Martha of Bethany has been long associated with hospitality, her sister Mary is connected to the soul that longs for Jesus's words. Mary sat at Jesus's feet, listening, soaking it up, digesting his words and hearing his heart. Mary was a seeker and a learner.

Mary's association may sound preferable to us. That's understandable. Martha's gift was very practical. Mary's was very spiritual. But it's more than okay to be gifted in the practical. If that's you, don't worry! God built you that way, and it's beautiful. But even those of us who are of a practical bent can use a little dash of Mary in our hearts.

What does that mean? Slow down for a minute. Take a breath. Don't allow every moment to be stolen by the drive to do, do, and do some more. Soak it in. Be filled with Jesus. Ponder his words. Turn your hearts toward God in prayer. Even if you have to set a timer to allow yourself this pocket of time to be free (without stressing about it), do it! The practical stuff needs to get done. But we must take moments for our hearts too.

Would you describe yourself more like Martha or Mary? Describe the reason for your answer.

Be filled with Jesus. Ponder his words. Turn your heart to God in prayer.

Day 93

But Martha was distracted by all the preparations that had to be made. She came to him and asked, "Lord, don't you care that my sister has left me to do the work by myself? Tell her to help me!" "Martha, Martha," the Lord answered, "you are worried and upset about many things, but few things are needed—or indeed only one. Mary has chosen what is better, and it will not be taken away from her."

LUKE 10:40–42

Ah, and here we see the downfall of "too much" hospitality. Martha was so concerned with doing everything that needed to be done while she hosted the large group of travelers in her home, she lost sight of the whole point—that *Jesus* was there and he was taking the time to teach them. She would have done well to sit at his feet and listen, just like her "lazy" sister.

The problem wasn't in too much hospitality, of course. The problem was in Martha's attitude. Jesus (gently) rebuked Martha because he knew her heart wasn't in the right place. She cared more about everything going well than she did about hearing Jesus teach. This was a rare opportunity, and Martha had the focus of an event planner, not a disciple.

Let's not get overwhelmed by the practical—or worse, in the temptation to show off. We have the opportunity to sit at the feet of Jesus metaphorically when we listen to his Word, so let's make sure we're present in those moments with our whole hearts.

What did Jesus mean when he said, "Mary has chosen what is better"?

Day 94

Many Jews had come to Martha and Mary to comfort them in the loss of their brother. When Martha heard that Jesus was coming, she went out to meet him, but Mary stayed at home. "Lord," Martha said to Jesus, "if you had been here, my brother would not have died. But I know that even now God will give you whatever you ask."

JOHN 11:19–22

Martha and Mary have now lost their brother, Lazarus, who was a good friend of Jesus. Martha ran out to meet Jesus to speak with him about it. Now, we may hear a little of that demanding nature Martha sometimes had. But really, this is a cry from an anguished, grieving sister—and it's a cry of faith.

Like the woman who had been bleeding for twelve years, Martha knew—just *knew*—that her brother could have been saved if Jesus had been near. If only Jesus could have prayed. If only Lazarus might have touched him. That's some big faith. But Jesus is in the habit of meeting his seekers and followers at whatever their level of faith and challenging it to expand further.

Martha said, "If only you'd been here!" and Jesus said, "I didn't even need to be. I can still act."

Does your faith feel small today? Or does it feel big and bold? Wherever you are, Jesus is ready to meet you and challenge you to go beyond what you thought possible.

Why do you think Martha could speak with total honesty to Jesus about how she was feeling?

Day 95

Jesus said to her, "Your brother will rise again." Martha answered, "I know he will rise again in the resurrection at the last day."

JOHN 11:23–24

Can all the Bible-loving, Word-studying ladies among us just take a moment to appreciate Martha here? Her theology was on point. She knew about the resurrection, understood it, and believed in it. You go, Martha!

It's not always the most inspirational thing in the world to talk about sound theology, but it's too important *not* to talk about. While different denominations will interpret the finer points differently sometimes, biblical, orthodox Christianity agrees on the essentials of the Christian faith.

Have you ever taken a few minutes to read your church's statement of faith? In all likelihood, it highlights these essentials, and it may even closely resemble one of the ancient creeds originally drafted by the early church, or perhaps one drawn up more recently during the Reformation of the 1500s and 1600s. Taking the time to dig into this history of church doctrine can help ground you in your beliefs. It may not sound super fun, but you might be surprised!

What comes to mind when you hear the word "theology"?

Day 96

Jesus said to her, "I am the resurrection and the life. The one who believes in me will live, even though they die; and whoever lives by believing in me will never die. Do you believe this?" "Yes, Lord," she replied, "I believe that you are the Messiah, the Son of God, who is to come into the world."

JOHN 11:25–27

Let's keep it very real: Martha's confession here was a deeper, better, fuller understanding of exactly who Jesus was than many of the disciples had until after Jesus had died and risen again. Martha got it.

It's sad that she's often remembered *only* for her shortcoming—her bad attitude about Mary not helping her. Martha was so much more than that. She was undyingly practical. She was a doer. She maybe cared a little too much about everything going perfectly. But her theology was sound. Her understanding of the Messiah—and her faith in him—was deep and real and true.

People want to put us in a box sometimes, just like they've

done to Martha for centuries. It's easy to think of people as one thing—the squeaky-clean church girl, the girl with the sketchy past, the sports girl, the bookworm. But we're all more complex than that and far more nuanced. We can't often control how others choose to define us. But we can make sure we don't pigeonhole people in this way. It's frustrating and unfair, so let's strive to see people for all their many facets!

What characteristics of Martha do you admire?

Day 97

Jesus, once more deeply moved, came to the tomb. It was a cave with a stone laid across the entrance. "Take away the stone," he said. "But, Lord," said Martha, the sister of the dead man, "by this time there is a bad odor, for he has been there four days." Then Jesus said, "Did I not tell you that if you believe, you will see the glory of God?"

JOHN 11:38–40

Oh, Martha. How can we not adore Martha? She just gave the most amazing profession of faith in Jesus as the Christ, but in the next moment, her concern is back to the practical matter of how decayed the body is and not wanting to expose the crowd to the offensive smell.

We have to love Martha because she's exactly like most of us—a mix of radical, earth-shattering faith and utter, hopeless density. Can't you just see Jesus shaking his head? Oh, Martha. If you believe, you'll see the glory of God. Here it comes!

Jesus says the same thing to us. If we believe, we'll see amazing things. If we believe, we'll draw close to the very presence

of the God of the universe. If we believe, we'll see eternity with Jesus. And we believe it—we need him to smack us upside the head with it sometimes too. Let's thank God that he's gentle with those rebukes!

How is Martha both a combination of great faith and occasional doubts?

Day 98

Then Mary took [expensive perfume and] poured it on Jesus' feet and wiped his feet with her hair . . . But one of his disciples, Judas Iscariot, who was later to betray him, objected, "Why wasn't this perfume sold and the money given to the poor? It was worth a year's wages." He did not say this because he cared about the poor but because he was a thief . . . "Leave her alone," Jesus replied. "It was intended that she should save this perfume for the day of my burial."

JOHN 12:3–7

Mary, our heart-connected, soul-seeking sister, did a beautiful thing here. Her perfume was obviously very valuable. And yet she followed the leading of God and poured it over Jesus's feet as a symbol of his forthcoming death and burial. Mary held nothing back from Jesus.

It's a stark contrast between Mary's heart and Judas's heart in this story. Judas sought to take all he could, even from Jesus's ministry. He betrayed Jesus for money—thirty pieces of silver.

It's hard to say exactly how much thirty pieces of silver would be, translated into terms we understand today, but in Jesus's time, it was the going rate for a slave. So, whatever the monetary value, Judas sold Jesus as no more than a slave.

Human nature often wants to lean toward a Judas mentality—to take, take, take—as much as we'd love to be Marys all the time. Let's spend a few minutes in prayer today, asking for more of Mary's generosity in our hearts and less of Judas's greed.

Why do you think that Mary held nothing back from Jesus?

Day 99

When Jesus rose early on the first day of the week, he appeared first to Mary Magdalene, out of whom he had driven seven demons.

MARK 16:9

Mary Magdalene's reputation has gone through a millennia- long game of telephone. Through pop culture references and word-of-mouth discussion about her, she somehow has the reputation of having been a sexually immoral woman or a professional prostitute. But the Bible doesn't say either of these things, only that Jesus cast seven demons from her.

How did her story get so mixed up? It's hard to say. We can only imagine how Mary Magdalene might feel if she were alive today and she could see what the common conception of her is. If you have ever been the subject of an untrue rumor, you can probably relate.

Having your reputation dragged through the mud is awful. There's no getting around it. But, like Mary might if she were alive today, we can rest easy in the knowledge that God always knows the truth. No matter what anyone else's perception of us

may be, God knows whether or not we fit the box we're being put in. While it's okay to defend our honor and speak the truth about ourselves, our ultimate comfort comes from the God of truth!

Mary Magdalene was the first person to see Jesus after he had risen from the dead. What does that tell you about Jesus's heart towards women?

Day 100

I commend to you our sister Phoebe, a
deacon of the church in Cenchreae.
I ask you to receive her in the Lord in a way
worthy of his people and to give her any help
she may need from you, for she has been the
benefactor of many people, including me . . .
Greet Andronicus and Junia, my fellow Jews
who have been in prison with me. They are
outstanding among the apostles, and they
were in Christ before I was . . . Greet Tryphena
and Tryphosa, those women who work hard in
the Lord. Greet my dear friend Persis, another
woman who has worked very hard in the Lord.

ROMANS 16:1–2, 7, 12

As we come to a close, if you have an extra five minutes, go read Romans 16. It's Paul's list of personal greetings as he signs off on his lengthy letter to the Roman church. This is a mere sampling of the names he lists, many of whom are women.

Phoebe is listed as a deacon, a word which is only ever translated as someone who serves that specific leadership role in the church. There is Junia, and while there are some alternate suggestions for translation, here the sentence strongly implies she was an apostle—not one of the Twelve, of course, but one of the outer ring of apostles leading the church. And then there's Persis, a woman who has worked very hard in the Lord.

These female church servants have one thing in common—they *do work* for Jesus and his church. Be empowered, beloved daughter, because you were created to be a change-the-world, make-your-mark woman. We've seen dozens of ways this calling played out for biblical women of centuries past. Let's walk in their footsteps and be the women we were created to be!

Among the list of women you've studied the last several weeks, who most inspired you?

Find More Awesome Devotions for Your Faith Journey!

Ditch the Insta-Perfect Pressure

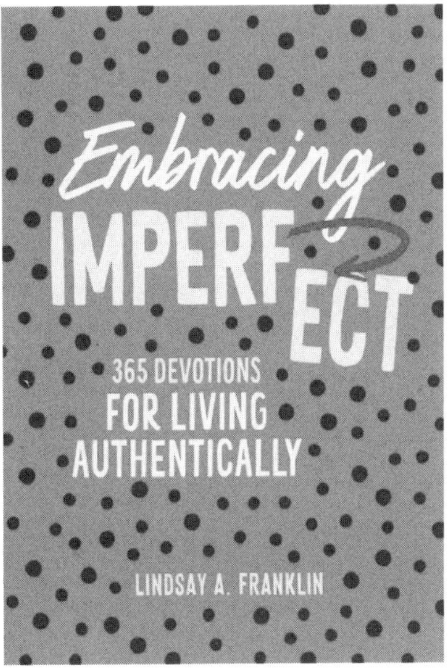

This year-long daily devotional will help you ditch perfectionism and self-doubt by embracing God's love for you, exactly as you are, through quick, Scripture-based reflections.

For free discussion guide download, visit Zonderkidz.com/Freebies.

Stress Less, Smile More: Your 10-Min Daily Reset

Chill out and boost your mood with these 10-minute daily reads that mix faith and real-life tips to help you stress less and feel way more confident and happy.

Your journey with God doesn't stop here! Check out these next.

Anxiety? Self-Doubt?
Find Your Security in Him.

This 100-day devotional will help you understand God as a protective Father so you can feel strong and secure while dealing with anxiety, pressures, and everyday life.

Social Media Stress?
Dating Drama?
Find Your Truth Here.

Feeling overwhelmed by friends, social media, or just life? Adored gives you a daily dose of truth and guidance for tough stuff, helping you find confidence and know you are infinitely precious to God.